Seventeen
Takes

Seventeen
Takes

Naima Kalra Gupta

RUPA

Published by
Rupa Publications India Pvt. Ltd 2017
7/16, Ansari Road, Daryaganj
New Delhi 110002
Sales Centres:

Allahabad Bengaluru Chennai
Hyderabad Jaipur Kathmandu
Kolkata Mumbai

Copyright © Naima Kalra Gupta 2017

This is a work of fiction. Names, characters, places and incidents are
either the product of the author's imagination or are used fictitiously and
any resemblance to any actual person, living or dead,
events or locales is entirely coincidental.

All rights reserved.
No part of this publication may be reproduced, transmitted,
or stored in a retrieval system, in any form or by any means,
electronic, mechanical, photocopying, recording or otherwise,
without the prior permission of the publisher.

ISBN: 978-81-291-4461-4

First impression 2017

10 9 8 7 6 5 4 3 2 1

The moral right of the author has been asserted.

Printed at Thomson Press India Ltd., Faridabad

This book is sold subject to the condition that it shall not,
by way of trade or otherwise, be lent, resold, hired out, or otherwise circulated,
without the publisher's prior consent, in any form of binding or cover other than
that in which it is published.

*To my mother,
the guiding force of my life*

Contents

Introduction   ix

PART I
1. Pier 42   3
2. Where Do I Go   16
3. The Fall of Izar   26
4. My Humble City   38
5. Will You Be My Friend   45
6. From India with Love   52
7. Into that Good Night   61
8. Sugar and Spice is What Makes it Nice   68
9. Manga to Bollywood   72
10. Evanescence   75
11. Not Belonging in the Game   81
12. Time to Turn the Page   85

PART II
13. My Struggle with Atheism — 95
14. The Indian Dream — 103
15. Irony of Privacy — 113
16. What Would Stalin Say — 120
17. The Age of Equality — 129

Introduction

From when I was a kid, I always used to read a lot. From *Nancy Drew* to *Harry Potter* to *War and Peace*, I have been across the entire spectrum of fiction. A few years ago, I started voraciously reading non-fiction too. What started as a hobby and a pastime soon turned into an intellectual pursuit (while continuing to remain a hobby). I started reading not just to be entertained but also to gain knowledge. Reading books started serving a variety of purposes in my life. It was a recreational activity, a scholarly journey, but most importantly it was solace. It was comfort and familiarity. I grew up with the characters in books, with words and with their love. And that is what I hope my book can provide people.

A collection of stories and memoirs, this compilation is definitely a coming-of-age book but not in the traditional sense. It's not about heartbreak or about enduring friendships and discovering alcohol and partying. It's about the the self. My book is remarkably self-centred. It's about the war that wages within all of us. Through the character of Izar I talk about some aspects of my own journey. Figuring out what to do with my life, lamenting the loss of innocent childhood, coming to terms with changing beliefs and ideals, developing new ideas with respect to my city, my country and God. I write about those ideas that very often are under-represented in teenage writing but are an essential part of who we are as children or adults. Each story contains some element of the truth, replicating in some ways my own life. I don't know how morally acceptable it is to speak the truth in fiction and to lie in non-fiction or what exactly the line between the two is. But if there was such a line, my pieces would fall in that.

Things that happen and people whom we meet when we are young and impressionable have a long-lasting impact on us. But the stories in my book aren't about that long-lasting impact or about how certain events in my life shaped me, they're about how they just clicked in that exact moment. For me personally, there are certain memories in my childhood that markedly stand out. I don't think about them every day, nor do they provide any significance in my day-to-day life, but they denote events that notably struck me.

An important thing I've learnt is that growing up is not easy. One underlying emotion behind all of it is frustration. You don't understand anything. By writing, to some extent I have been able to channel what I feel and give some coherence to my thoughts. I don't write to change the world. Romantic though that notion is, I don't believe that it is the purpose of literature. That isn't the purpose of art in general. Thrill and bubbling excitement are the two recurring emotions I feel when I come across great art. Being able to produce that euphoric feeling, I believe, is the primary purpose of this activity.

I started writing seriously around four years back but honestly the process began much before that. It's not just about the stories you type out for an audience, it's about the little thoughts that are constantly developing in your head. From my silly poems that I wrote as a kid, trying to forcefully rhyme words, to the diary I kept as an adolescent, to my blog, and now to my book, they're all stories within my story.

We've all had books we've read in which we can relate 100 per cent to the character or to the author, if not throughout the story, at least in parts, and we've also had characters with whom we couldn't relate at all but we still ardently loved and admired. While reading a book, which may be familiar or may be exhilaratingly new, the reader embarks upon one line or phrase that moves their world a little. It doesn't have to be profoundly meaningful or grand, but it's so elegant, a breath of fresh air, that it seems the entire book was worth it just for that one line. That is the experience I want to be able to give to my reader. As long as one aspect, even one line of my book, makes someone see something completely differently, gives them something unique, it will be the most rewarding experience for me as a writer.

I have read countless books; I can't say that I remember every story because I don't. But I do know that the lines, the bits and pieces that I do remember are the most important parts of the book for me. Some authors make you fall in love with their words. That's a grand ambition, one I'm probably far, far away from, but that's the place I wish to be.

The first few of my stories are through Izar's (the protagonist of the story) perspective.

'Pier 42' primarily deals with the question of who we are and what do we want. As people, this existential question has and always will haunt us. In simple words, 'Pier 42' is Izar's struggle with trying to answer the question, 'What is the purpose of life?'

'Where Do I Go' is a question that Izar asks herself. Now that she's grown up, she reminisces about her childhood. Although she knows she can't go back to those good old days, she's trying to figure out where it is that she can go next.

'The Fall of Izar' is about conceit and obsession with one's self, and despite some guilt over the same, Izar finds that she can't help but think of herself as superior to others.

'My Humble City' and 'Will You Be My Friend' are both stories of how two girls had a profound effect on Izar. They didn't 'change' her or influence her deeply, but they were both people she admired and who possessed qualities she wished to incorporate, which was unusual for the self-righteous girl that she was.

'With India From Love' is about Izar's love for her country, India. As someone who wasn't always patriotic, Izar comes to redefine what that word means for her and realizes her new-found love for the country that raised her.

Success feels great. Obsession with it, however, isn't. Every kid has felt the desire to excel and the overwhelming feeling that comes with intense competition. 'Into That Good Night' is a story that narrates Izar's experience with success and her subsequent realization that failure isn't the end of the world.

The Part II section of the book deals with a variety of social issues.

'My Struggle with Atheism', as the title suggests, is a struggle with atheism. In a country as religious as India, being non-religious, let alone an atheist, is not easy. Religious tolerance includes not just Hindus, Muslims and Sikhs, but also the forgotten and ignored atheists.

A widely discussed yet highly relevant topic has been the parents' obsession with science. 'The Indian Dream' tries to combat the detrimental bias towards the subject and resulting neglect and stigma against the humanities and related careers.

Are we completely safe anywhere? Probably not. On the Internet? Definitely not.

'Irony of Privacy' talks about why, although it seems we are anonymous on the internet, we are in fact more exposed and vulnerable than ever. The need to be cautious on the internet is more important than it was ever before. The Big Bad World, thanks to the internet, just became 'Bigger and Badder'.

You versus world? Who should be picked? The ethical, political and social dilemma of trying to decide whom to prefer, the individual or the community, is one that is essential in order to have effective policy and social welfare programs. 'What Would Stalin Say' weighs the pros and cons of one against the other.

Casteism and reservations are one of the most controversial and hotly debated topics in Indian politics. 'The Age of Equality' provides arguments as to why reservations and other measures of upliftment are needed to mend what has been a broken system. We need to correct the errors of our past and make amends. It is after all a new age, one of equality.

The other stories deal with forming new friendships and learning to deal with the end of old ones. Moving on, insecurities and fears are things everyone, teens in particular, have to deal with.

Part I

chapter 1

Pier 42

The only way to deal with an unfree existence is to become so absolutely free that your very existence is an act of rebellion.

—ALBERT CAMUS

'Whoa…watch out,' says Keiran, as I stumble on the edge of the pier. Pier 42. I'm standing barefeet with my feet against the warm cemented ground. I look down at him for a second, then throw my head back and laugh—a cocky, condescending laugh. My mahogany hair, grown over the summer, grazes my waist. I settle down beside him, lean back and rest myself on my elbows.

I point a finger to his chest. '*You* should know better than to warn me. After all, I am Izar Savannah Hollister,' I say to him. Then I laugh again. I scrounge around for pebbles to throw in the water.

Laughing, Keiran faces me, 'And that doesn't mean shit.'

'Sure it does,' I grin at him as he takes a puff of his cigarette.

Kieran is tall and lean, with an adorable mess of brown curly hair. He looks older than he is, even though he's clean shaven. He's always dressed casually in shorts and a t-shirt. The most formally dressed I've seen him was when he wore jeans and a button-down shirt at his parents' anniversary party last year.

I throw the pebbles in the water; it's awfully choppy today.

Keiran exhales and looks at me. 'What?' I ask.

'How are your college applications coming along?'

The stone splashes in the water.

'Why on earth would you bring that up?' I grumble.

'Oh I don't know. Maybe because it's right around the corner and also potentially life changing. They say you get a job if you go to college; you might want to consider it,' he says with raised eyebrows and a mock-serious expression.

'Cut the sarcasm,' I grumble even more.

He stares at me expectantly.

I sigh. 'I don't even know if I want to go to college. Seriously. I know I have to, but I don't know if I want to anymore.'

He looks straight ahead at the water, 'Why not?'

I shrug my shoulders. I seem to be doing that a lot lately. 'It seems kind of pointless, doesn't it? You know I want to learn everything under the sun, but is four years of institutionalized learning with a price tag of $20,000 really worth it?

'Heaven knows it's not. But those in hell highly recommend it.'

'Yeah, well, I have always had a thing for Satan.' I pout.

'So?'

'I don't want to go.'

'So don't go.'

I look at him and huff, 'Yeah, right.'

He crosses his legs and sits up straight. 'Izar, listen to me. No decision till today has really been yours. No one asked you if you wanted to be born. You weren't asked before being sent to school. And now you don't have a say about going to college. Your life has pretty much been mapped out,' he says. Then he leans in closer, his breath smelling of smoke, and whispers, 'If you ask me, that's the saddest thing I've ever heard.'

I stare at him again, 'I choose not to have a choice. I could decide to do anything I wanted. But I don't. Because for me, maybe, the risk isn't worth it. I do what I want to do and you know that. If I really don't want to go, then I *won't*.' I enunciate each word as stubbornly and emphatically as I can.

He shrugs, 'Sure you make decisions on things that don't matter every day. You'll choose what college you want to go to, what career you want to pursue, who you want to get married to. If you decide to, that is. And these decisions will just delude you into believing you're in control. But are you really?'

I take the cigarette from his hands, take a drag and sit up straight. 'Delusion, my love, is the only thing in this world that keeps people like you and me sane.'

'But how delusional are we really if we know we're delusional?' he says slowly, with a cocky smile.

I smirk at him. 'Oh wow! A paradox.' I say teasingly. 'Kieran's become smart. Who would've thought you're that complicated?'

'Only a fool wouldn't have,' he pauses for a second. 'Maybe the fault really is in our stars. We just like to believe it's not. Because if it's all already written, then we're just puppets waiting for the strings to be pulled. And that doesn't sit well with us.'

I snort, 'Of course it doesn't. Humans and their fragile egos. But you know some would say that's a weak approach, surrendering to fate.'

'Oh trust me darling, I'm not. I'm just saying maybe we're all just delusional. And everyone knows fatalism is the inferior ideology,' he jokes. But then he looks ahead at the water again. I know he's really thinking and his mind is somewhere else right now. 'Who cares about who's at the steering wheel anyway? The captain thinks it's him, but actually it's the wind.'

'Maybe so,' then I lean in and he looks at me, 'But tell me, isn't *control* the only thing you've ever really wanted?'

We stare at each other unflinchingly—a battle of dominance.

Don't try to pretend you understand me.

But I'm the only one who gets even close.

Whatever.

He looks away. Snapping the connection. And we sit in silence, leaving the evening wind to make small talk with the waves.

I'm seventeen years old and I have the rest of my life to look forward to. And when you're that young, it isn't often that you find yourself with deep regrets. When you're living in the 21st century, where people chastise conventional thinking, it is not often that you find yourself wishing that you could choose a different path in life. I haven't even chosen one yet, though Kieran would say that maybe I have. That maybe there is nothing to choose. Most days I'm bored. There is this energy that I do not know where to channel. Kieran helps keep me entertained but I know he's just as bored as I am.

We're both in our last year of school right now. And for all our talk, neither of us actually has the guts to drop out. We're stuck, at least for a year. We talk about how this stuff isn't for us and we pretend to be way more problematic than we actually are; it's a product of our inflated sense of self-worth. Gee, no wonder we get along!

But I can't help finding myself lost in the pages of the future that I have written for myself. I always did, naively, believe the angelic illusions that fiction fed me. And I feast on them now. The reassuring whispers of these dreams are like opium—making me hallucinate about a kingdom of possibilities. The problem, I should mention, is that no two dreams I visualize are the same. Every fantasy springs from a different source, like they were not mine but different people's desires. I don't want to ask myself the over-used, over simplified, cringeworthy question, 'Who am I?'

If I was stuck on one idea, if it was just one utopia that glided like a ghost in my dreams, night after night, I might have become obsessed enough to make my life mirror these euphoric visions. But when arrays of dreams come in flashes, changing constantly, when I'm so overwhelmed by looking at a million pictures at once, I wonder which one I like the best. So I ask myself, what do I even want from life? I don't come up with nothing; in fact, I come up with too much. Maybe these are my childish endeavours, maybe I'm too caught up in realities that exist for no one but me, or maybe I'm just crazy.

Adults around me tell me I need to grow up, that I need to get my life in order. But I cannot deprive myself of these doses of unexplainable euphoria I get when I take a trip to fantasy land. It's who I've become.

The evening comes closer and we start walking back home. The wind continues to blow my hair, and I wrap my arms around my waist. I try to synchronize my steps with Kieran's but it's hard since he is twice my height, and two of my steps equal one of his. He snorts at my feeble attempts to hurriedly keep up with him.

In that moment, I am happy. But I am also unsettled and have excess energy. There's this urge to play with fire. So I ask him, 'Do you think we're going to make it?'

'If I could bet my money on anyone, it would be on you, Izar. But I don't know about myself.' He pushes his hands deep into his pocket.

'You're kidding, right? Tell me one person in this world you'd want to trade places with? Wait, I'll tell you. *No one*. And I wouldn't either. You and I, we love ourselves too much, we have too high an opinion of ourselves to ever want to be anyone else. And in that sense we've already made it.' I say with a self-satisfied smile, proud of my discovery on us making it.

I see his little brain turning and processing my 'radical' theory. 'Well when you put it that way... I never really thought about it like that.'

'Yeah, that's probably why you need me. You never think about anything, right?'

'Pffft whatever.' He rolls his eyes. But it's an affectionate gesture. I shake my head and smile to myself.

We walk quietly for a bit. Nothing is ever as comfortable as silence between us. While most people fret and fumble when words cease to be spoken, we connect better when we can only hear our own thoughts. But Keiran seems exceptionally lost today. Usually it's me. I have a tendency to get so lost in my own head, that I zone out for hours. What's better than my own company, right? Sorry I'm just being full of myself. But today it looks like Keiran is the one floating in the clouds.

After a little while Kieran says softly, 'Izar?'

'Hmm?'

'Don't go,' he says quietly.

'Don't go where?' I ask him even though I know exactly what he's talking about.

'Don't go to college in the States. You—'

'Keiran,' I sigh, 'We've talked about this. You know what my stand on that is.'

'No listen to me. What's the point? You yourself said it, you don't even really want to go,' he says urgently.

'I said I don't know if I want to go or not. And I did really want to go six months back. I don't know what I'll want in another six months.'

'Who cares? This is elitist and not you. Don't go.'

I'm pissed now. It's not his decision and he doesn't know what I want. *Brat.*

'I can't act on every little whim I get. Look where that got you.' I say.

'What does that mean?' There is an almost dangerous glint in his eyes. I have managed to get the fire started.

'It means you don't have a clear plan Kieran. School finishes in less than a year, what are you going to do then? You've been jumping around from one decision to another.

Or should I say from one indecision to another.'

'I don't have a plan because I don't know what I want, Izar. I'd rather do nothing than do something completely arbitrary.' He enunciates each word with force.

'No. Don't lie to me. I see right through that. You want a plan. You don't have one and you're scared. Don't give me the "take life as it comes" story. I know it's complete rubbish.'

He doesn't look at me and his jaw pops out.

I start my full rant. 'You're scared. Just admit it. You don't know what's going to happen and as much as you want to go live independently in the real world, you have no clue how that's going to work out. And that just scares the living hell—'

'Fine, Izar! You got me all figured out. Congratulations!' he is half-shouting now. He storms ahead. Suddenly he stops dead in his tracks, and turns back. He holds my shoulders and looks me straight in the eye and says, 'I might be scared. But so are you.'

I'm not afraid of him. That's why we work. I give it right back to him. 'No, I'm not. You know I'm not. So stop trying to make yourself feel better by bringing me down with you.'

He runs his hand through his hair, 'Oh my God, Izar! You think that's what I'm doing? Because, let me spell it out for you, my bet is on you. If anyone's going to make it out, it's you. And I know you're not scared. Not about this. Dammit! I envy you for that! But you *are* scared. About one thing. You want your life to mean something. And you don't know if your perfect life in an Ivy League will give you that. And that scares the shit out of you. You think I don't see you struggle every day, trying to wrap your head around everything you do. Tell me, Izar, why would someone with a life as perfect as yours complain at all? Because you don't want to be a poster child. But you also do. And that internal war—it rips you up.'

I stare at him. Then I smile. Cold and hard. 'Now that was a fascinating conspiracy theory, wasn't it? Did you come up with it all on your own? Maybe you can write a book about it.'

No one says a word after that. We walk back in silence. Only this time, it's not as comfortable.

I pace back and forth in my room. No sleep for me tonight, I suppose. It wasn't that I didn't already know what he said. This wasn't some great epiphany that happened to me today. But the question was, how did he know? Was I really that easy to see through? For as long as I could remember, I'd been a model student. I had near-perfect grades, I was smart and I knew it—I was great at my extra-curriculars, teachers loved me, I had a pretty good profile. But more than anything, I was focused. I knew what I wanted, I knew how badly I wanted it, I knew how to get it, and I did what I had to, to get it. The only problem was that it changed. I lost track of what I wanted. Suddenly I realized that if I wanted a perfect life, there were a thousand other things I couldn't have. But more than that, suddenly, it seemed that there were things that were more important than my own fickle existence. Things that were larger than life.

The one thing, the only thing that haunted me night and day was how do I bring meaning into my life? Should I spend my life in servitude to others? Or should I make a lot of money and become powerful? Was I supposed to just lead a simple life? What was the correct path? The moral one? Was it possible or was I condemned to a mindless existence? And how, for the life of me, was I ever to figure that out?

I meet Kieran on the way to school the next day.

I put my hands in the pockets of my shorts and go up to him.

'Hey, you.' I nod at him.

He looks at me.

'Hey,' he says crisply but not entirely hostilely.

'So,' I drag my words, 'How's it going? How've you been? All good? You look chipper.'

'Cut the small talk, Izar. It's not for us.'

'Fine,' I take a deep breath. 'Okay, so I've been thinking about what you said and maybe you're not completely, outrageously wrong. I just don't have anything to say about it. I mean what can I really say?'

He sighs and his face softens. 'It's okay, you don't have to. I get it. I got carried away, but I'm not sorry for saying what I did.'

I give him a small smile, 'I know you're not. Look I don't

understand what goes on in my head. I don't understand what goes on in your head. As much as I hate accepting that, it's true. Also if the human brain was simple enough for us to understand, we would still be stupid enough to not understand it.'

'What?'

'Jostein Gaarder said that,' and I repeat what I had said. 'Basically we can never figure ourselves out, as much as we want to,' I add.

I can see his brain processing what I just said. It's weird I can always see and hear him think.

'Our whole lives we try to figure out the purpose of our existence. Maybe that's exactly what our purpose is,' he finally says.

'Maybe.' I lean into his shoulder.

'Whatever, this conversation is messing with my head,' he says shaking his head. Seems like Philosopher Kieran has retired for the time being.

'Life is messing with my head,' I say.

I feel his body rumble with laughter.

'We'll write a book one day, you and me.'

'Philosophy at Pier 42' I tell him.

He laughs again.

'You're kind of a dork,' he says kissing the top of my head.

'Albeit, a smart one. A really smart one.'

'Showoff! Go learn some modesty please.'

'You know what they say—it's not bragging if it's true.'

I say with a full smile.

From philosophers to five-year-olds in two seconds, this is our relationship in a nutshell.

He laughs, and starts to say, 'You know for someone as short as you, you sure do have a lot of spunk.'

'With good reason.'

'Really, what reasons?'

'I can start listing them for you if you want. For starters, I have really good taste in movies. I also have great hair. Did I mention I am smart, like genius smart? Also I can eat more than you. That gives me a lot of bragging rights. I can—'

'Stop,' he says exasperatedly but not without love. 'I got the point. Meet me at the Pier this evening?'

'I'll have to think about it.' I wink at him. 'The Pier makes you kind of grumpy and sullen. All that attitude of yours comes up. Maybe it's the salt water. Or the wind.'

'Please, just stop.'

'You know I love teasing you.'

'Please go away to college. Right now.'

'Careful what you wish for, mister,' I smile. 'You never know. It might just come true.'

chapter 2

Where Do I Go

I asked my soul: What is Delhi?
She replied: The world is the body and Delhi is its life.
—MIRZA ASADULLAH KHAN GHALIB

Delhi, they say, is the city no one expects to fall in love with, but everyone does. They don't say that. I do. Ask me what I dislike about Delhi and I can give you a concrete list. It is a list of obvious things. I hate the crippling poverty I see every day when some beggar knocks on the window of my car—with nails caked in mud, oily mousy hair, sick thin arms and ribs poking out so sharply, I'm afraid the skin will rip. I hate the intolerance of Delhi-ites as they scream and shout the most scandalous cusses and get into fist fights over the most mundane things. I hate that I live in the most polluted city in the world, where every breath I take is like puffing a cigarette. I hate that a hundred-rupee note is all it takes to convince a traffic officer to turn a blind eye to drunk driving. I hate that after two minutes of taking a shower with ice-cold water, I am again drenched in sweat because of the sweltering heat. It goes on. But this list is finite. My grievances, surprisingly, are indeed finite.

I've lived in Delhi all my life and I like to think that I understand her. A big city with small-town people, with bustling cars and hundreds of pedestrians, with mansions next to slums, with no house remotely similar to the next, with spotless houses and filthy streets, with majestic trees and garbage on the ground, with 'No Honking' signs behind trucks whose drivers are responsible for tremendous noise pollution. The city of juxtapositions. The city of contradictions. But who can claim that they in themselves aren't a contradiction. I know I am. Delhi might be the capital of a 'third world' country, it might not be the most advanced city in the world, its people might not be the nicest but they have something to offer that no one else does. Delhi-ites get what they want; they possess an almost stubborn reluctance to accept that anyone else might be better than them; they're strong-headed and bold. Poverty does not disgust us. And despite everything, despite knowing that the child beggars on the streets are part of a ruthless industry, many Delhi-ites keep food to give out in their car.

I don't see myself as an Indian as much as I see myself as a part of this city. It is a city complicated to understand, its machinery is a direct metaphor of the human mind. Of my mind. I see myself in every action. I will never get bored just walking around the city, just looking. In fact, I will always miss out on seeing something. Everything, well almost everything, I have ever seen, ever experienced, has been here. The city taught me to read between the lines, it has taught me that people aren't just people. But Delhi just is. She just goes on and on, doing her own thing. So much happens, but nothing stops her. She just goes on. I can leave and never come back, but she won't stop. Not for me, not for anyone, not for anything. And every morning I think to myself, the day I halt my world, or the day I let anything stop me is the day I cease to be a Delhi-ite. The day I cease to be me.

There are things I've always been and there are things I'll always be. I've always been a girl of places. I get attached to places: cities, houses, areas, streets, anything. I've always associated myself, my identity with the intricacies of the places I've been to. A flicker of my soul, a 'ghost of Izar' is still roaming in every place I've been to. Someday, I like to believe, I'll go back and collect it. I'll collect what that ghost of mine has acquired through the years. This belonging, this connection, I suppose I feel most ardently with Delhi. Delhi, or rather Dilli, is my soul. There is no city I love more fiercely than Delhi. And the ghost that I will leave behind here, won't be a fragment of my soul, it will be my soul. But I have to leave her. She is not the woman you marry. She is the woman you come back to. To fully embrace her, to fully understand what she's done for me, to fully understand how much she has embossed herself in every fibre of my being, I must leave. If only to come back. She's the city no one expects to fall in love with, but everyone does. She's not perfect. And she doesn't need to be.

She holds in her hands the countless places that have raised me. And tonight I go back. I go back to collect.

The grass is moist like it always used to be. The children are still there like they used to be. The night is young like it always was. But my steps are hesitant like they never were before. Tonight I go back. I go back to my childhood, to those days that seem like a lifetime ago. I was the most happy-go-lucky child. I loved life. When I think of the days before I entered middle school, I only remember sunshine. I lived in a land where the sun never set. And then, I grew up.

This field is where I used to skate every day. I started taking skating lessons when I was four, but somewhere along the middle, I stopped. I'm not sure why. Probably like every child, I got bored. I probably insisted and my mother reluctantly gave in. I wish she hadn't.

Coming back here feels good. Better than I thought it would. This skating rink was such an important part of my childhood and I had forgotten all about it. I think it's weird that you go through every day without thinking about so many things. They just lie there, at the back of your mind, waiting to be remembered. And then in some random moment you regain consciousness about the existence of this memory, and it's like you remembered all along. I owe it to this place to come back.

It's chilly and I wrap my cardigan tighter. I walk across the football field. The rink is at the corner of the field. It's dark but there are two rustic lamp posts at the ends. Small flies cluster under the light, buzzing. From far, the rink looks luminous. I come closer and I see children skating. I remember the feeling—like I could fly. Of course I didn't think that then, but I can feel it now. It's weird, you know. Reality is always better than expectations, a memory is always sweeter than the reality really was, and reliving an experience is better than a memory ever served.

Today I want to go back. Into a much simpler world. I don't call my childhood simpler, I call my child-self simpler. I wasn't such a complex web of emotions and feelings, woven by opinions and judgement. I was free from the shackles I tie myself in. Now, I don't know how to go back. And coming here doesn't help, simply reminds me that I grew up.

When you read a book, after a while you forget the small details, but you remember what it was about, what the story was. Now when I look back, I can't remember all the small details. I'm sure I had my low moments. But now I can just see an upward graph. From far you don't see the small breakdowns, the lows, but the steadiness and the overall picture. Have you ever seen an intricate drawing from a little far? It looks lovely. But when you peek in closer, you can see the faults and the imperfections. But the picture is beautiful.

And I painted that picture.

My name is Izar. I was born in Delhi. All my life I've lived here, but I still don't understand the city. I remember my mother taking me for Christmas carnivals, and plays about magic and mythology. I remember going to book fairs and to art exhibitions. I remember when one good thing ended, another followed close behind. Today I find myself holding on to every piece of happiness, I cling to it like a child clings to her mother, scared that I'll get lost. I don't remember the city being so harsh. I don't remember the rapes, I don't remember the politics that scarred us, I don't remember the crippling poverty, the dirt and the terror. Maybe I just didn't know. Maybe I can still ignore what I've seen, what I know. But how much longer can I live in limbo, suspended between reality and imagination? I'm not a child anymore.

I turn to Kieran and say, 'Kieran, you remember this place? Remember I brought you here once?'

Kieran only smiles at me. As if I'm a child.

He's my best friend. I've known him since I was four, but we became close only later. Kieran's the kind of person you can't help but be drawn to. When he's in the room, he's like the sun and everyone else just helpless sunflowers. Wherever he is, people are automatically drawn towards him. He has that compelling power. But once you get to know him, the way he thinks, the way he talks, you realize that the most beautiful part about him isn't his ability to draw people, but it's his mind. He looks at the world in a way no else ever has. He's a mystery to those who know him, and ordinary to those who don't. Or maybe he's just a mystery to me. But I know him better than anyone.

Now I look at him and I see the difference. He's become much taller. His lanky frame as a preteen has now emerged as broad shoulders. His eyes, his eyes are the same. Warm and sad.

I turn to look at the children skating. I wonder if this is just another after school activity for them. I wonder if they only come because their parents tell them to. I wonder if I used to be like them and when this place became significant for me.

Kieran was always good at judging my mood. He always said the right things. As he does even now.

He puts his hand on my arm.

'Izar, it's okay. This place means something to you, and it's okay if it doesn't to them.' Kieran says softly, 'We all have our havens we want to go back to. This is yours.'

'I miss it. That life, that sunshine. But I don't even remember it. It's hazy and all I can remember is the bright light.'

'I know, but we have to go,' he says, tugging my arm.

I didn't know what he was talking about. I was tired of leaving. I wanted to start going back. I felt that ghost of my past come back to me. She embraced me fiercely, gripped my arms and shook me, as if asking me where I'd been all this time.

But if I don't turn to my past, where do I go?

Arzoo, like Kieran, has been my friend for as long as I can remember. I can almost remember us being little girls, with my long wavy hair reaching my waist and her blunt bob, wearing skirts, with pudgy legs, hair bows and our little hands locked in each other's.

Every time I went to her house we used to go to Lodhi Garden. The Mughal influence was heavy, but of course as kids we didn't notice or care about that. We were more concerned with being able to play hide and seek at the fort. Yes, the fort. Qila. Only later did we realize that it was a tomb. Technicalities were beyond the point. We saw this archaic red stone structure with pretty architecture. It looked mysterious and adventurous and that was pretty much all we cared about. Adventure.

As seven-year-olds, the tomb held a sort of magical appeal to us. It was dark and dusty, made of red sandstone, and, in our imagination, the 'house' of ancient kings and queens. Raniyon ka mahal. I loved playing pretend. It was my favourite game ever. I'd always had a hyperactive imagination—from make-believe friends to a non-existent sister. So naturally when it came to playing, board games and stuffed toys didn't suffice. I needed imaginary characters and stories. Maybe it was the feminine instinct in me or I just wanted to pretend to be grown-up, but I particularly liked playing house. Arzoo and I used to fantasize about being adults living together in our own apartment. And of course, most importantly, we needed fake names. Maybe because we were Indian kids charmed by the West, we always chose to keep 'white' names: Savannah, Katie, Destiny, Alex etc. And since Arzoo and I were only two people, we obviously needed to have more characters in our little make-believe world.

'Elena, that's Mike right there and he's my husband.' I don't know what fascination we had with getting married. 'Where's Alex?'

'He's standing right next to you. How about we all go out for dinner?'

'All right, Arzoo—'

'Elena, Elena, Elena.' That was the biggest mistake. You always use given names.

'Yeah, Elena, we'll be running a little late because we have to go for Amaya's (fake daughter?) piano concert.'

'That's not a problem. I'll probably be late from work too. My boss is super strict.'

I just nodded in complete seriousness.

Now that I look back, I can't help laughing at how we were so gullible and so desperate to grow up. But now I'm desperate to go back to that age. I would give up anything, anything in the world if it meant I could go back in time. And this time, stay there. I wish Arzoo and I could be back in Lodhi Garden—rolling down the hills and getting our clothes covered in freshly mowed grass. We always regretted it later because the grass would make us itch for hours. But we did it all over again anyway. It's memories like these that bring a bittersweet smile to my face. But right now, when

I'm back in these gardens, with the majestic Peepal trees gazing at me with pity, I feel a lump rise in my throat. A lump that I know will remain just that. I won't cry. The place that tears come from is bleeding dry. And this lump is worse than even a waterfall of tears because I can't cash in on my misery. I can't let it out. It's stuck in the hollow of my throat, blocking all air and literally choking every whisper of joy from my body. I don't know or understand why I'm so sad when I'm so young. I feel my shoulders sag from responsibility as Atlas's did. Like him I can't relieve myself from this burden. My arms are trembling and my eyes are blotched with red, but for momentary relief I take trips down memory lane. Trips to sun-kissed gardens and cool breezy summer nights at the rink. This is a sweet madness. But when I run out of places from my past, when I run out of happy childhood memories, when I reach the end of my darling Delhi, when I'm at her outskirts, then where do I go?

chapter 3

The Fall of Izar

The road to hell is paved with good intentions.

'I'm sorry,' I whisper in a barely audible voice. 'I'm so so sorry.' In fact, the only evidence that I'm speaking at all are my moving lips. My fingers come up to touch my lips. I see my hand move. My hair is spilling over my shoulders, my skin is pale under the white light and my eyes are wide open. But when I look in the mirror, everything is out of focus except my eyes. I stare right into myself.

Two weeks ago, Inayat called me.

'Oh hey!' I answer cheerfully.

'Hey Izar, how are you? It's been a while,' she says.

'I know, tell me about it.'

'So I was wondering if you want to hang out at Arzoo's place tomorrow? Just us girls?'

'No man, I'm sorry but I really can't come.'

'Why not?' The disappointment in her voice is obvious.

'It's just that I have too much work to do, with applications and everything. It's a tough year. But we'll meet soon?' I try to sound as optimistic as I can.

'It's okay. We'll find time. You take care,' she says.

'Definitely, bye!'

Click.

Next week I get a notification.

Inayat liked a picture you were tagged in.

A picture of me at a party with other friends. Friends that aren't her or a part of the rest of our group. She doesn't say anything to me. It's simply not who she is. I know if our roles were reversed, I would have gone up to her and demanded what had happened to 'too much work'. But she never said a word. Like it never happened. I almost wish she had confronted me.

I wipe my tears, and looked at my mascara-smeared hands. I stare straight ahead at my reflection. My lipstick is smeared, my eyes are blotchy and streaked with red, my dark circles obvious, and my hair a mahogany mess.

I ask the girl in the mirror, 'Oh what have you done?'

'It's not too late.'

'Is it not? My life's a colossal mess,' I ask incredulously.

'They still love you. Just talk to them. You can do that, you know that, right.'

'They probably hate me. I would hate me.' I squeeze my eyes real tight. 'I do hate me. Oh! What am I going to do?'

'Are we still friends, Izar? Do you even want to be friends with me or am I just throwing myself at you?' She's hyper. Her hands are on her hips.

'Of course not. I've just been going through a lot.' I try to appease her, playing the pity card.

'I know you have.' Her voice softens a little. 'But you just cut me out. Why?'

'I didn't.' I try denying it, even though I know it's true.

'Listen, if you don't want to talk to me, or if things have changed for you, then just tell me. I'll go away. But I just want you to know that they haven't changed for me. So don't leave me hanging.'

'They haven't changed for me. And come on, Inayat. If I haven't been talking to you, it's not like you've been talking to me either. Don't put it all on me.'

'Izar,' she says, 'I did try. You were the one who was too busy with your new friends or with Kieran.'

'Why didn't you ever come up to me? And ask me? I waited. I wanted you to come. But you didn't. You never called once or even texted. I just thought you didn't care. If roles were reversed, you know I would've come up to you. I would've asked you flat out "What's the deal?" But I guess it is just easier to pin all the blame on me.'

Just like that I turned the tables. I turned them so fast that she didn't even understand what was happening in this whirlwind. In a second I put it all on her.

The tears are dried up. I can't pity myself any longer. I

am a manipulator. Maybe I've always been this way. Even as a child I used to emotionally blackmail my friends to get them to do what I wanted them to do.

'Am I really that cold? Why don't I ever accept responsibility?'

'You are, right now.'

The sanctity of friendship was lost to me. It seemed that I could not value relationships anymore. But it wasn't a lack of love; it was a lack of respect. I was sifting through friends almost as fast as I was changing clothes.

'Nothing is sacred to me. I always overstep boundaries. And most of the times, I don't even regret it. I'll end up dying alone.'

'You can make friends in hell. There'll be your kind of people there.'

'Oh shut up.'

The mirror shuts up.

Even with Keiran, I'm on his case, with no respect for how close we are.

'Why do you have to argue with me on everything these days? You're starting to annoy me.' He sounds irritated.

'Well maybe you should stop making unfounded statements. If you want someone to agree with you on every illogical, nonsensical thing you say then you can go talk to one of your dumb girlfriends.' I'm even more irritated than he is.

'It's getting really annoying, you know. You fight over

everything. Why do you love controversy so much?'

'I'm the devil's advocate,' I clarify.

'Whatever man, Izar.' He rolls his eyes. 'Talk to me when you're over yourself.'

That was exactly why I argued. People were starting to irritate me. It was the same story every day and I couldn't deal with it anymore. Everywhere I went, everyone was just stuck in their own rut, repeating the things that irked me no end.

Inayat and Arzoo could not stop with the gossip. It just went on and on, and the more I heard it, the more my blood boiled. Don't get me wrong, I liked my fair share of 'Who-kissed-who' news, but all the time? Give me a break.

'Oh my God! I have to tell you something. Did you hear? Laila and Faisal broke up again.' Inayat started off.

'What? Really?' Arzoo's excitement was almost sickening.

'Yeah, I just heard yesterday. Apparently Laila was crying in school. She just wanted to create a huge pity party for herself. Who does that?'

'She is so stupid, she never even realized that Faisal was just using her.'

Stop. Please.

'Did you see Sheila's Instagram post last night? What was she even wearing?'

They both giggled. Who giggles?

'Haha! I know, right. Girls are weird, man.'

Excuse me. So are you. Please get a life.

'Wait, Izar, I'll show you.'

'Guys, come on, stop, do you ever talk about anything but other people's lives? Unless she was parading around town naked, I don't care what she was wearing to a stupid goddamn party.'

They look at each other sheepishly.

'Never mind. I'll catch you guys later. Have fun stalking girls on Instagram. Real purpose to your lives guys.' I don't know why I get so worked up. It's not my business and I need to hold back on the judgement. It's not like I don't gossip. I just can't help myself from calling them out on this.

Things were equally bad with Kieran.

'If I actually put in effort, I could beat anyone at anything. I just don't try. I could easily get better grades than you,' he tells me one evening on the Pier.

'What? No, you couldn't,' I snort.

'Trust me I could.' He's serious.

I can be serious too. So I say, 'Fine, let's bet on it.'

He shakes his head, 'No man I don't want to bet on it because if I do then I'll have to work hard and I don't really want to.'

'Well, maybe you should try proving yourself, not that you'd be able to beat me.' I tell him.

'I just don't see the point of doing the work, so I won't. But that doesn't mean that I can't.' He insists and he insists. Why is he arguing with me on this?

'Please stop annoying me. Let's not talk about hypothetical

situations all right? "If I actually try" and all that. If you actually had brains or guts, you would've agreed. The day you do something, we'll talk then. For now, you have no reason to be conceited.'

'You're such a brat. It's not like you're any less conceited. You've just never been around someone who could actually challenge you and you can't stand the thought of me beating you.' He sounds self-triumphant.

'Stop using the word actually. Saying it again and again won't make what you are any more real. You can't beat me and that's a fact. You're not even willing to take a challenge so please take your ego and your baseless conceit and get lost.'

'No, that's not a fact. It's your opinion and what the hell is wrong with you?' He's frowning at me.

'What the hell is wrong with you?' I say raising my voice.

'I'm done here.' He raises his hands.

'That makes two of us.'

Pretty much all my friends are starting to get on my nerves. It was just the same story every day. And I know it's me and not them, with the attitude problem. It didn't take more than a few months for people to lose their lustre. All that glittered, glittered for only a bit.

I was happy to have an excuse to fight with everyone. To keep my distance. But there was just one thing that seemed to be my enemy. Guilt. I felt bad.

'Maybe you really are a brat, Izar,' I grumble at myself.

I stare at myself. And 'mirror me' stares back at me.

'A spoiled, ungrateful brat who got everything easy.'
No reply.
'An obtuse selfish brat with narcissistic tendencies.'
No reply.
I can't even bring myself to lie to myself now.
I squeeze my eyes shut and two more tears fall down.
These aren't sad tears. They are tears of frustration.

'Why are you crying? It's not like you miss them, you heartless creature. And this pity party you have thrown for yourself right now, this isn't about them either. It's about you. It's always about you. You are heightening your own importance in their life. You feel guilty for being a jerk. Because that's what you've been recently, haven't you? A jerk. Your tantrums and your whims. You make everyone tolerate them. Then in one moment of some self-actualization, you realize how much attitude you have been throwing around and then you wonder why they don't put up with you. You tell yourself it's because they love you, and they know that you love them. You tell yourself that you do a lot for them. That at the end of the day, you're the better friend. That's not true. I'll tell you why they put up with you. It's because you're a bully. You've coerced everyone into believing that you, Izar, can get away with this. And you do get away with it. But the problem is, you feel guilty. You're feeling guilty right now. There is that little conscience pricking you inside. Nagging you. You want to be a better person. No amount of beauty or brains or charm can compensate for that. The problem is you think you're on a pedestal and till you continue to stand on that pedestal in your illusions, you will continue to act like you're the monarch. You're not a queen darling, and your friends aren't your subjects. So stop your act. Let your feet touch the ground and leave the halo for real angels.'

And thus my Shakespearean monologue ends.

'You're scary, you know.' A new friend of mine tells me.

I laugh, 'That's definitely not the first time I've heard that.'

'You can be really intimidating when you want.'

'What? I'm so polite and nice though.'

'You're scary. Plain and simple scary. "I don't want to mess with her" scary.'

Why are my friends scared of me? This is not how it is supposed to be. Friends aren't scared of friends. Bossy. Bully. Intimidating. Scary. Is that how people see me? Is that how my friends see me? I guess they will only see what I show them. But do I really make a conscious decision when I put up the face that I do? Do I get to choose what I show them or does it just happen?

I won't say that around people I'm not the so called, clichéd 'real me', because I don't believe in a real me. When I can see myself change every second like the turning of gold mechanical clocks, when I can hear my thoughts change rhythm and pitch, when I can feel my emotions dissolve into nothing and be reborn like a phoenix, then how can I ever talk about the real me. There isn't a real me. There isn't only one me, the face I keep up is part of who I am, the lies I tell are a part of the choices I make, the secrets I keep are a part of my insecurities, the smiles I fake are a part of my fear. So it's not about the real me but it's about the 'all of me'. It's probably multiple personality disorder. Quite feasible at this point. But seriously, you don't show the all of you. To anyone. Ever. It's against the rules of society. A lady never reveals her secrets.

The ticking of shoes, lace and silk gowns grazing the marbles floors, music and chimes lapping at people's ears, tightly laced corsets, jewels in the hair, bow ties and cologne, faces hidden beneath glittering Venetian masks. Sway to the music, talk in hushed tones, but don't let the mask come off. It's a masquerade ball.

Identifying yourself, trying to find your own voice, getting to know yourself and finally coming to terms with who you are, are some of the toughest challenges anyone faces. It's a constantly evolving realization, which springs up on you at the most unexpected times. The facade we struggle to keep up, the desperation behind the efforts we make, the smoke of the lies we tell, and the stench of the pretence that evolves us, how do we learn to see beyond it?

But more than that, will we really feel comfortable with letting anyone see what's behind the mask? And how do we know what the mask looks like? To see the mask ourselves, we must take it off and in the process, expose what's behind it. Sometimes I wonder what if people get to know how I think, will it be similar to how they think, will they find a comfortable place among my thoughts, or will they be pricked by them? Will they glide through my conscious or will they stare with repugnance? I sit here and wonder, but I don't have the courage to invite anyone to see beneath the surface. The crust is me, the inside is me too, but people only judge and see what's on the surface. Few can and few want to look beyond that, and I don't blame them. It's easier to live on the surface of the ocean, where all is calm. Dive deeper and you see the seaweed, the turbulence, the flailing mud and yes, along with that comes the risk of drowning, but it's also in the heart of the ocean where the marine life flourishes, where a potpourri of colours light up before your eyes. All treasures, they say, lie at the ocean bed, but who is willing to go that deep. No one wants to unravel anyone. It's risky, it's scary and it's unknown territory.

We say we know people but we don't. We say we get them, but we don't. We say we're there for them, but how can we when we don't know what they're going through? I'm scared. I want to tell them. But the fear of judgement will always surpass the need to express myself. We all love the glitter on our masks.

I can tell you that I, Izar, love my mask. When you let people in, you need to have respect for them and you have to be on the same level as them. I act on my whims. I do as I please. Guilty though I feel sometimes, my guilt is temporary. It's definitely not powerful enough to make me act otherwise. The insecurities, the fears, the vulnerability, they are never going to surface. That's not what this is about. It's not about what's underneath the surface. It's only about the surface right now.

I look in the mirror and I don't see the mask. I like being intimidating. I like the power that comes with it. I like being called a brat. I like that no one but I know what's going on. I love my pedestal. I like being the monarch. This rush or power I get, however imaginary it is, I love it. And that is the problem. I don't loathe or hate any of the wickedness that is there in me. I have too high an opinion of myself. Why? I don't know. I even love the fact that I'm conceited. And I love the fact that I love that I'm conceited. And so on. You see where I'm going with this cycle. I love every dark corner of who I am. But unfortunately this love does not extend to other people on this scale. I love myself too much. And maybe that will be the fall of Izar.

I quote Nietzsche to myself, 'If you gaze long enough into the abyss, the abyss will gaze back at you.' Maybe I'm the abyss. I definitely think I'm sophisticated enough to be quoting Nietzsche. I'm kidding no one, it is sophisticated. My conceit does have a few boundaries.

The abyss is staring back at me.

'I love myself.'

The mirror shatters.

chapter 4

My Humble City

*It is very often nothing
but our own vanity that deceives us.*
—JANE AUSTEN

She had a thing for cities. They spoke to her, especially at night—high rise buildings, towering skyscrapers, billboards, neon lights, crowded streets, the buzz and most of all, the people. The people were at the epicentre of the energy that cities were charged with; a charge that flowed through her. She was a city girl through and through. She lived the fast life, ran the rat race and kept up the appearances. She had inhabited every characteristic that made a city a city, every characteristic that made her, her. There was one characteristic in particular: Arrogance.

The funniest thing about city people is that they can't see through their own arrogance. It's so entwined in their upbringing that they don't notice it. To be fair, everyone around them is more or less the same, so they feel no different. Every aspect of city life cultivates this exact vanity, this entitlement. I was talking to a friend once and she said we're brought up with an inherent sense of entitlement. We're the best. We deserve the best. We can be the best. It is our right. So much so, that I just talked about myself in third person. And truth be told, I love the sound of it. It wasn't long before I was called on this arrogance of mine. Not by anyone else but by myself. Me again. I suppose that's my arrogance playing up.

Human psyche, I soon realized, was a funny thing and something one shouldn't think about much if personal sanity was valued. But despite my better judgement, I do wonder about how we function. Or more particularly how I function. It is, after all, all about me.

Last year I was at summer camp when I met a girl, Sahana. She was from a village about two hours from Delhi. I say this because that's the moment I realized just how much of a role 'city life' had played in sculpting me into who I was. I realized I definitely had pretentious and narrow worldviews and I wasn't even at Harvard or Yale yet. This wasn't some grand epiphany or an 'aha!' moment. It was just one encounter. It did open my eyes, not in the dramatic Bollywood sense, but in the sense that it gave me a broader perspective into how much background really mattered. It's funny how people like me have such strong political and social opinions when we live such sheltered lives.

Soon enough, I was obsessed with her. It is a little dramatic. Maybe it was that allure that paupers always hold for princesses; the small town charm, the romantic appeal of the simple life. Her demeanour, her laugh, the way she carried herself, the way she spoke to and about people—I was intrigued by everything she did and said. Spellbound. Every conversation of ours was just me asking her an array of questions. My questions just never ended.

'What's your school like?'
'Favourite subject?'
'Where do you live?'
'What's your family like?'
'Do you have siblings?'
'Do you get along with them?'
'How's boarding school?'
'What do you want to do when you grow up?'

To most people these might seem like questions to make polite conversation and kill awkwardness. But for me, they really weren't. These weren't conversation starters or social niceties I was indulging in. I genuinely wanted to know how her day-to-day life functioned. Each question of mine had a follow up. The more I learnt, the more I wanted to know. Simplicity and humility, it seemed, fascinated me. The best part is that for every question I had, she had one for me too. She was reciprocating my interest.

I was from a big city. She was from a small village. I was decent at basketball. She was great at basketball. I spoke

English and Hindi fluently. She spoke Hindi mixed with Haryanvi (a local dialect). I watched chick flicks and crime serials. She watched old Hindi movies. I was spoilt. She was grounded. I drank only bottled water. She drank anything which looked clean. I texted and tweeted. She sang songs. I liked fine dining. She liked her mother's home-cooked food. We were both focused and wanted to do well in life. We both liked math. We both found pleasure in simple things (she a little more). We both liked helping others. We both liked each other. We both dreamt big. She was a small town girl who wanted to make it big. I was a privileged brat who wanted to make it big. Yet, it still seemed that her odds were better than mine.

The very fact that I could look at her with such appreciation is testimony to how, for once, I set my 'I, Me, Myself' attitude aside. Sahana made me realize that the mirror I had held up for myself, was by no means accurate. I felt like I was in rags in a five star, naked in a church, overdressed at a party—I was out of place. Suddenly I was conscious of my own habits and whims; my demands and my extravagant style of living. I was conscious of my attitude, and how hard I worked. If I worked hard, I felt that she worked harder. If I had a fire to excel in me, I felt her fire burned brighter. If I put others before me, I felt she didn't put herself anywhere at all. If I was humble, I felt her humility made me look boastful. If I was happy-go-lucky, I felt she made me look sober. She was better than me. I accepted it.

I didn't resent it. I loved it. If my mother saw it, the shock of it would've almost given her a stroke.

I have always been particularly critical of people. I look at people, scan them for faults. I may like people but I will still be aware of their faults. Sometimes it takes me time to be able to look past peoples' flaws. But Sahana was a person I couldn't find faults with. If anything, she made me find faults in myself. Imagine that! I looked at her without judgement and only with respect. I'm not a love struck girl, fangirling over a boy band. But I might as well be. That's the affect she had on me.

She was sweet. She got excited if I gave her my yogurt at lunch. If there wasn't enough space, she was the first person to sit on the ground. I never heard her boast. Not even once. At night, she got sad because she missed her family. Looking at her cry, I almost cried. She didn't complain. About anything. How do you do that?

Pride, I feel, comes before fall. But for me, I think I was lucky enough to meet someone who made me realize how unnecessarily proud I was. Not that I'm not anymore. I just became aware of it. And most of all, the futility behind it. In school I had always despised the people who thought money, material and social standing were everything. In front of her I realized how blinded I had been. I judged those people, but realized that what they say is true. Don't judge people without looking at yourself first. She, who had every right to judge me, to look down at me and at those other people, didn't. She embraced me with open arms, wanted to know about me, wanted to help me and was truly kind to me. I felt materialistic in front of her. I felt I was transparent, while she was a solid rock.

Meeting her was a reality check, a look into my inner self. It was time to get off the high horse I was riding. In the grand scheme of things, I am just a girl who is barely any good at basketball, has decent grades and thinks that she is the pinnacle of morality. I think I am always so right, but am I really so great if I can't see my own flaws? She made me see who I am, and who I can be. She made me realize that I am not better than everyone else until I accept that I am the same.

She was so much better than all of us, but she didn't need anyone to say it. She didn't even need to think it. In fact, she didn't. She just was. I think all of us get so caught up in ourselves that sometimes we forget to see our mistakes. Being self-confident is good and she was. She had the kind of confidence I never did, but she seemed so humble and grounded. She knew exactly where she stood. It's time we find out too.

On the last day of camp, Sahana hugged me and had tears rolling down her cheeks. In that moment I realized she wasn't just someone I looked up to but someone whom I had ardent affection for. In many ways she was a child. She was two years younger than me. Her naivety and disbelief at the realities of the world amused me. She couldn't believe that people cheated. She couldn't believe when someone did something bad. And I loved her innocence. She was wise and young at the same time. Camp ended and I never saw her again. We haven't been in touch. There are times when I think about her and wonder where she is and how she's doing. I feel like she thinks about me too sometimes. Or maybe that's my conceit playing up again. I want her to think about me. I miss her sometimes. I hope for her sake, or maybe more for mine, that she never changes. That she remains just the way she is. The world could do with more people like her. My city could do with more people like her.

I walk on the city roads. There's always something happening. The pollution may not allow you to look at the stars, but there's enough around here to look at. The city isn't safe at night. Pity, since that's when it's at its best. The city is arrogant too, you know. Not just its people. The 'metropolitan', 'cosmopolitan' nature. The neon lights. Oh! they're the essence of our arrogance. But sometimes, just sometimes, the city needs to bow to the village.

chapter 5

Will You Be My Friend

*If you don't know where you're going,
any road can take you there.*

—LEWIS CARROL, *Alice in the Wonderland*

In 2008, when I was nine years old, my family took a cruise to the Bahamas. That is one trip I remember very distinctly; the gigantic, vibrant polished water slides; the shining aquamarine colour of the pool on the deck, the mini golf course with multi-coloured golf balls, the grand feasts of never ending food, the thousands of desserts—tiramisu, banofee pie, fruit cream pie, key lime pie, strawberry tart, apple crumble, chocolate fondue, Oreo cheesecake, everything chocolate. Then there were the shows put on every evening with Venetian dancers, circus acts, acrobats, burlesque, music and comedy, the treasure hunt, ice statue carving competitions, sporting tournaments and bingo. It's safe to say I was as enchanted as Cinderella was by Prince

Charming. While all these luxuries did create a pleasurable vacation, the details are completely fuzzy in my head. After all it was just another vacation we took. But there is one thing about the trip that I significantly remember. Actually one person: Elizabeth.

The adults usually checked me, my sister and my cousins into the Kids' Club, so that they could go do whatever it is that adults do; usually just drink Bloody Marys by the pool side. I was happy with this arrangement. I couldn't have been more excited to do every fun activity they had lined up for us in the club—from playing toilet paper soccer and capturing the flag to face painting, hula-hooping and making our own toothpaste. It was the coolest thing ever. I was a fairly social kid, so making friends wasn't an issue for me either. I loved playing with other children, discovering new friends whom I insisted I had life long bonds with. So soon enough, I became friends with Elizabeth. She was two years older than me. I still remember she was so dignified, mature and funny. She was fun. I just so badly wanted to be best friends with her; to be the one she paired up with for all the fun activities, to have her laugh at all my not-so-funny jokes, to have her confide in me, and go eat ice cream from the ice cream machine together. If she was going to eat vanilla-chocolate mixed, then so was I. But there was more to the story than her just being the coolest person I had ever met.

So one day her parents came to check her in and they

were white. Caucasian. But Elizabeth and her brother were brown; they were Latin American. Obviously this baffled me. Little though I was, I understood something was up. I was a surprisingly sensitive child and not wanting to be rude, I didn't ask her what it was about. But that didn't stop me from being curious. Like I said, she was mature and dignified, so she told me her story. Oh boy! Her story piqued all the interest my nine-year-old self could muster. She was one fascinating person.

Those were her adoptive parents. They had adopted both her and her brother. In fact, she had another stepbrother who was in Kids' Club too and he was Asian. Then she told me she had multiple brothers and sisters, all adopted. Her adoptive parents had two children of their own who were now grown up. She and her brother were from Mexico and her biological parents had given them up for adoption because they didn't have the money to support their family. Their new parents had been travelling to Mexico, where they met them. They'd been adopted two years ago. And then things happened and before they knew it, Elizabeth and her brother were part of one big family. Every year her adoptive parents, being exceedingly wealthy I assume, would take a trip with a couple of their children since they were too big a family to travel together at once. I'd never heard anything like this before. When I first got to know I just wanted to sit down and cry. She couldn't live with her mommy anymore, and her parents had willingly given them up in exchange for money. I gained some solace in the fact that at least she had her brother with her, whose name I cannot remember. Let's call him Albert. Albert was reserved. I never got to talk to him. Of course at that age kids stay away from members of the opposite sex unless you're related to them. But I felt sad for him and I wanted to talk to him. Elizabeth, on the other hand, didn't seem sad at all. From whatever I understood, she was pretty happy. She seemed content with whatever life was. She didn't have hang-ups and even though she looked mature to the little Izar, when I look back I realize that she was only eleven. As much as her story enthralled me, I grew a genuine liking for her. Okay, maybe that's a little bit of an understatement. I practically hero-worshipped her. I was happy being her little tail. And that, might I add, was quite uncharacteristic for me.

I was short and tiny, and I guess being around a lot of new kids made me a little shy. I was one of the younger kids in the group and there was this one white girl, Emily, who decided to pick on me. Quite characteristic for white people; they have been picking on us Indians since the 1600s. I wanted to be friends with Elizabeth and so did Emily. So, a not-so-friendly-and-healthy competition developed between the two us. But I'm telling you, she started it. I can proudly say that Liz liked me more and it was obvious. That must've burned a little. So Emily started picking on me and bad mouthing me to Elizabeth. I don't remember the details but I remember Liz stood up for me. Indians for the win! That was probably my first experience with something like that; the first time a friend took me under her wing. I was an unusually bossy child. Back home, among my peers, I used to assume the role of a leader or a tyrant, some might say. I used to tell everyone what to do, the girls in my class needed my permission to do a lot of things—like what sport to play, what to get on the days of the class party, what other girls to talk to, and so on. There hadn't really ever been someone whom I wanted to be *friends* with before—someone who I looked up to, and admired. It's safe to say that I, Izar, fell in love with her, Elizabeth.

Of course other than thinking she was perfect, I felt for her. I wanted to offer her solace. This is probably my earliest memory of having such complicated emotions. I was still a short skinny girl with long wavy hair, a baby voice and missing front teeth. I don't know exactly what effect it was that she had on me, then or even now. But she's just someone in my memory who stands out. I didn't meet her for long, just a few days. I don't even remember saying goodbye to her. I just remember her. She was all limbs; tall and bronze with medium wavy light brown hair. Although I wouldn't be able to recognize her today even if, by some chance, I meet her again.

I remember telling my parents all about her, to the extent that my mother remembers who she is till this date. There are a few people who enamour me, but once they do, I'm hooked. Maybe it was the short span that makes it's seem more theatrical than it would've been. In fact, I'm glad that I knew her for just a bit. I'd rather not lose the charm and glorified image that I have of her right now. This, I feel, is something I do often. I let my imagination make a memory way sweeter and dramatic than it probably was. The problem is, that now this is the only way I remember it. Or maybe it's not such a problem.

I think it's funny how there are some people you meet every day and you probably won't remember them five years down the line but then there are some that you meet just once and remember them forever. Maybe she was just an ordinary girl. Maybe she wasn't. But there is at least one person who remembers her and wonders what she's doing. I'm wrong. There's definitely more than one person. There's someone else. Her parents. They probably think about what she and Albert are doing every day. Do they regret the decision they made? Or are they happy their kids have more opportunities now? For some reason, I really want to know. Maybe one day when she earns enough money or grows up, she'll go visit them. Maybe she won't. I don't know why but I really hope that their parents get to see the two of them again. Even if it's just to see that they're doing great. I feel emotionally connected to this family that I have no connection with. It's weird.

Was it her sob story? Was it just her personality? Was it the fact that she was my first older friend? To be honest, I don't know. It could've been all of that. She definitely doesn't remember me. Surprisingly, that doesn't make me very sad. With Sahana, it had been respect and love. She'd taught me something. But with Elizabeth, it was just idolization. Maybe I was a loser kid. I tried to please her, get her to like me, to play with me and be my friend. She was more special to me than I was to her. It was definitely an unbalanced friendship. Her story gave me my first glimpse in to the real world. It was something I'd just read in books before. My heart went out to her. That was it.

I had the time of my life riding down those waterslides, splashing into the clear water, putting those ridged golf balls, stuffing myself with pastries, watching spectacles and playing bingo. But it was within the four walls of that Kids' Club room that I got my first exposure to what I'd like to call the real world. There were real people there who experienced some very real things. My initial shock and gradual amazement makes this girl stand out in my memory.

'Hi, I'm Izar, will you be my friend?'

chapter 6

From India with Love

*It is lamentable that to be a good patriot
one must become the enemy of the rest of the world.*

—VOLTAIRE

Nationalism as a concept always intrigued me. But it was something I never associated myself with. I was never a patriot. I never wanted to do something for my country. I was one of those who believed that people were people. Humanity was humanity. For me everyone was equal. Indian, Chinese or British, how did it really matter? After all, weren't we taught from childhood that countries were nothing but man-made boundaries? Artificial differences that people had created? Mankind, I believed, was one. Many a times this belief of mine got me into conflict with a lot of people. Patriotism, it seemed, flowed in the water of this country. 'Incredible India'. 'Bharat Mata ki jai'. These ideas were absurd to me. What about India was incredible? Was everyone blind? Granted we had a rich culture and history that seemed almost unparalleled. We are a diverse lot. But so what? Our freedom struggle was glorified, creating images of heroic battles and noble victories in our mind, all derived from concepts that ran in every Indian's heart—Ahimsa and Swaraj (non-violence and self-rule). Our forefathers had sacrificed blood and sweat to make us free. If such was the case, if we Indians were indeed so inspired by Gandhi and our heroic past, why did we seem hell bent on proving to the world that we Indians are now nowhere close to being anything close to what our nationalist struggle was? Was it our slums, our crippling poverty, our lack of morals or our intrinsically corrupt nature that made us Indians incredible? Is it our pious politicians or our dutiful citizens, that give the impression that India is incredible? Must be both. Patriotism was a delusional concept in my world. One that sought to spray Chanel N° 5 over a reeking dumpsite. How much of the stench it really masked, I do not know.

India is a country of hypocrites. We preach what we will never practice in a thousand years. We pride ourselves on being moral and religious. Let's see what it is about us that can stand witness to us being moral? Is it our outrageously low sex ratio? The rates of female infanticide? Honour killings? Is it the urine on the walls that talks about our greatness? Oh right my bad, must be our high levels of religious tolerance. No wait; it's definitely child marriage. Corruption must be it. Don't get me wrong, I fully appreciate the fact that every society has its set of social evils. I'm not talking about India in particular here. Every country prides itself on something or the other, completely ignoring the long list of problems that do exist. If every country is better than the rest, then I see a little conundrum. Someone's going to have to take one for the team and call themselves the second best. We just can't have that many 'greatest nations'. Well at least America is waiting to become great again. Patriotism in this sense is detrimental. Its entire basis seems to be to avoid tackling problems. We just keep celebrating our nations, but for what? What is it that we are celebrating?

I've always been attracted to the dark side. Satan was my first love. Soon enough, the radical in me began questioning the notion of countries. The world would be a better place without countries. I'm not talking about one Supreme Leader of the World, that's too Alexander the Great. I'm talking about erosion of nationality. Morally speaking, we are one people. Why create distinction based on governments? Because there is only one thing that is tying a country and its people together: Government. These boundaries are fickle. India and Pakistan were one, until one day we split. Suddenly all love was lost. The USSR split up, and suddenly people living in Russia don't love people living in Uzbekistan? It's incredulous. Is patriotic love that fickle? More often than not, people living near the borders are culturally more similar to the neighbouring country than to someone living half way across their own country. People living in Darjeeling are more Nepalese than they will ever be Indian, but hey it's the Modi government that unites us.

Rationally all these ideas appealed to the radical in me greatly. I liked the notion of global citizenship. I liked to think that I had a realistic idea about what India really looked like. An objective point of view. 'I'm not really patriotic,' I told people around me. Yet there was this one thing at the back of my mind that baffled me completely. Something that I just could not understand and, as a result, completely ignored. My love for my country. It was irrational. I could not, for the life of me, explain why every time the national anthem played, my heart swelled with pride. The elated feeling, the rise in my chest, the rush that mouthing 'Jana Gana Man' got me, was inescapable. I loved singing our national anthem, and it's not just because I liked the lyrics. I could not explain why amidst hundreds of people from different countries I was drawn to Indians. This 'irrational' attachment I could not explain. I got defensive when I read an article against India. Why?

The nationalist movement itself, and our freedom fighters changed the very notion of patriotism for me. They changed the way I looked at India. Studying history, *itihas ke panne*, the pages of history, took me back into the epicentre, the heart of Indian patriotism—the Indian Independence Struggle. The young Congress members of the time—Nehru, Bose, Vallabhbhai Patel and Maulana Azad held an undeniable appeal to me. These were highly educated, well-groomed men; men who had dedicated themselves to the nationalist cause with nothing to gain except the well-being of the nation. They didn't go around shouting 'Incredible India!' they didn't campaign about the greatness of our country. No. What they saw was injustice, their own people suffering, plight, denial of basic human rights. It was this distress of the people that moved them to act. They wanted to bring about a change, they believed in their cause and so they did something about it. This, in my eyes, was pure honour. Why is politics today such a sham? Why are Indian politicians today widely disliked by their people? Why were politicians in 1947 adored? Granted they got the country free. But it goes deeper than that. They weren't just politicians; they were social reformers. For them they were their country and their country was them. They weren't there to serve themselves, they wanted to serve the country and for most of them, it was one and the same thing. Patriotism, I realized, wasn't this obscene outrageous belief that my country is the best. It is this burning desire to make it the best, this conviction that no sacrifice is too big when it comes to India.

I learnt that justice was the heart of patriotism. That changed everything for me. Maybe you can say it's about how you interpret this idea, but my interpretation changed. All my doubts about ignoring social evils came to a screeching halt. Patriotism wasn't about shouting slogans; it was about tackling problems in your country. 'My country, right or wrong' became 'Make my country right'. However, one of my biggest dilemmas, something that I'm still trying to come to terms with, is why should I serve India in particular and not just the world as a whole? After all, like I said, people are, at the end of the day, just people, Indian or otherwise. Maybe there is an irrational element to all of this. Why do we have more affection for our own family? Blood? We've known them forever? Our country is our family. Its citizens my brethren. Maybe it isn't quite as natural or biological as a family, but it is close enough. Love has never been rational. This does not mean that if one Indian and one English man were dying I'd choose the Indian. No. A life is still a life. But every time I stand with my back erect, my face stoic, and my lips mouth 'Bharat Bhagya Vidhata', I am reminded that I am Indian. India is my country. I do believe that I am human first and Indian second. People will come and people will go. The very concept of a country might die out in a century. The idea of India might collapse like the British Raj did. The words of the national anthem might be forgotten, but serving people, bringing about change will never die out.

Humanity might be humanity. People might be people. But some people are my people.

Maybe my love for my country stems from some scholarly interest and affection for the rich history that this nation can provide me with. But culture has been an equally important part. I have always been attached to my heritage. That has been something that I have very intimately tied my self-identity and upbringing to. From the epics like Mahabharata that my parents used to tell me as bedtime stories, to the lights of Diwali—each and every part of my culture is something that I am very closely attached to.

Although I'm non-religious and an atheist, I love Diwali. This has been something that has been consistent from when I was a little girl. More than the festival itself, the build-up to the day was what I enjoyed the most. The entire city just lights up. There are lights everywhere. Neon pink, blue, white, yellow—every house is draped in garlands of lights. It's typical for each house to do up their lights in an atypical manner. There are flowers, decorations, rangolis, embellishments...it's as if the city is truly ready for Ram to come. Suddenly the air smells different. I'm not trying to be dramatic. The mithai, flowers, smoke, all make up this concoction that smelled distinctly festive and to be more precise, distinctly Diwali. But more than anything else, I loved the celebration. Everyone seemed happy. As naïve and childlike as that sounds, it was precisely the pure unadulterated joy of this festival that made it special for me.

The first thing I used to do after waking up was wear my lehenga. Eventually my mom would talk me out of wearing it so early, warning me it would get dirty during the preparations. Disappointed, but realizing that she was right, I would reluctantly go change.

'Mom can I please, please, please start decorating the flowers?'

'Daddy can you please take me to buy the colours?'

'How come we haven't put up any lights yet? It's almost Diwali.'

Yes, I was the festival police. Everything had to happen under my watch. No one could slack. It was Diwali after all. This childhood excitement has translated in to my life now. Diwali is still my favourite time of the year and for me it is still the most beloved part of my Indian culture and upbringing.

One of the most exciting aspects for me was the Ram Leela. It was art, culture, music, Diwali, mythology, all combined in one. A two-hour spectacle that brought everything I loved together. My entire family used to go, sit in an outdoor amphitheatre. I could barely contain my bubbling excitement and the euphoric rush that this time of the year seemed to give me. It was a musical, most beautifully put up. I can never appreciate any other interpretation or variant of the Ram Leela. For me that was the absolute.

My love for Delhi, Diwali, butter chicken, lehengas, street food, Bollywood, all tied up into my sense of belonging. This was what I grew up with. These were the things I associated most of my good memories with. I am a daughter of this country. This culture, my values, my tastes, my upbringing have been carefully crafted by every aspect of Indian life. I had never fully accepted my Indian-ness for the simple reason that I was against the very idea of nations. It has been through studying the history of my country that I have learned to truly embrace India. My greatest epiphany has perhaps been to realize what it really means to be Indian. Being born in this country did not make me Hindustani. India made me Indian.

chapter 7

Into that Good Night

*All your life you wait,
and then it comes,
and are you ready?*

—ANTHONY DOERR, *All the Light We Cannot See*

2015

It's just sheets and sheets of elegant symbols and cursive letters, written in royal blue ink, sprawled across my lime green desk. My solutions aren't quite as perfect as I'd like them to be. The proofs have minor glitches in them, here and there. I'm almost done with solving all the questions. There are only ten after all. I'm almost ready to submit my application. Almost. I go over the proofs again. Each q.e.d ('which is what had to be proved'), my own personal victory. This is it: my shot at math camp. I don't think there are enough number of times I can review my work. I have to stop now. This is my opportunity to spend four weeks doing intense math. Or maybe it's my opportunity to prove that I can achieve something. To prove that I'm smart.

'So how's the progress on your problem set?' my friend Arzoo asks me.

'Oh it's fine,' I say brushing her off. I don't really want to talk about it. I can't imagine how I'll face everyone if I get rejected.

'Well you don't need to worry for a second, you'll get in,' she assures me and pats me on my back.

I don't want to get into it again and explain to her exactly how competitive it is and how smart the people who apply really are. So I just smile at her and shrug, 'I guess we'll just have to see.'

Flash forward two months and the email is sitting in my inbox. The fate of my 2015 summer is written in it. The fate of my self-esteem is sitting there. And my internet won't work. The email won't download. There is a venomous snake coiling in my stomach, becoming tighter and tighter by the second.

I cannot believe how dramatically climactic this scene is. I don't need the suspense to build up anymore. I'll burst.

Again and again I tell myself. 'You're not getting in. You're not getting in. You're not getting in.' Trying to lessen the impact. 'It's okay. It's completely okay. It's a highly competitive program. You can deal with rejection. You're prepared for rejection. It doesn't mean anything.' My inner voice is on a rambling streak. They're all lies. I play it again and again.

Broken record. It's a comforting yet unnerving methodical cycle. Like the clicking of a pen.

The internet connection is back.

'No false hope Izar. You'll only be let down. You're not—'

'Congratulations! We are pleased to inform you…'

What, did I just read congratulations?

I read it again.

Congratulations. Congratulations. Congratulations.

Pleased. Pleased. Pleased.

These are good words. Positive words. Surely they're not congratulating me for not getting in.

My clockwork brain is spinning. The information is being processed. The wheels are turning, I can feel them. Then suddenly I can't breathe. It hits me.

Oh my god. Oh my god.

I got in. I actually got in.

My world was spinning and I was enjoying the ride. I wasn't clutching on to the bars holding on for dear life. I was rumbling with laughter, my hair was flying and adrenaline was pumping in my veins. And I was high on success.

I don't know what to do with my life.

Maybe there was someone out there who deserved it more than I did. Or maybe this was what I had earned on my own. Maybe luck was on my side. Maybe I had overcome obstacles. The truth is in that moment it did not matter. That moment was mine, and mine alone. And I have tucked it far away from dark thoughts that lurk in the shadows of the night, away from the snarky comments of others who don't understand, and away from the predatory eyes of those who want to bring me down. In that moment when my heart jumped out of my throat, when my hopes spilled out of their jars, I was in a place that didn't exist in this universe. Getting into this program isn't my claim to fame. It does not define who I am or what I can do. It is simply a reminder that I can be who I want to be. It is hope wrapped like a trophy.

I am Izar. A girl whose dream just came true. It is ordinary, because dreams come true every day. Sometimes we're at that point where we're holding on for dear life, and our eyes are clenched shut. But amidst this moment we must remember that roads can turn any second, and then will come the time to laugh and to enjoy the ride. Dreams are not who we are, they don't segregate us into losers and winners. They're accessories that gently nudge us to keep going on.

2016

For the past one year I have been trying to come to terms with new things that surround me. Like history, the course of my beliefs, my values and my ideology has changed on multiple occasions. I see my thoughts maturing, developing as I pocket new experiences and see more of the world. By world I don't mean only geographical places, I mean exposure to new realities, harsh discoveries and different possibilities.

Reader, let me give you a brief account of how my own

beliefs changed. It began with the desperation to get into an Ivy League school. Drawn to the brand name, to the glamour and certification of an Ivy League, college was always at the back of my mind. I became obsessed with the idea of an Ivy. If at that moment someone told me all my chances were gone, I would have probably taken the blow really hard and suffered from clinical depression. Such was my condition.

I had previously mistaken my crazy obsession as intense passion. Something to be proud of. Slowly I became aware of the poison I was brewing for myself. So I started toying with the idea of not getting into a top school and being okay with that. It was a difficult meal to digest. But slowly it sank in. I knew I'd be disappointed but I'd survive the blow.

But this didn't change the fact that my short term life goal was still to get into a branded school. The perfect scores, the perfect essays, the perfect application, the perfect answers, I was preparing to strike perfect. In more honest and less eloquent terms, I was trying too hard. I was desperate and I reeked of desperation.

More recently as I have thought about this, talked to different people, weighed in the consequences, the less I care about brand schools. Now, here is where comes in the faint line between not caring and not letting it be the driving force of my actions. I've taken the reins into my hands. This realization or enlightenment or salvation or whatever you want to call it, came about for a variety of reasons.

Firstly, I slowly realized that these universities were

overhyped. They are not palaces and I was not a princess. They are oceans with so many fish that you get lost in the swarm.

Secondly, I realized that I wasn't weak enough to be controlled by some imaginary admissions officer's wishes. I wasn't going to live my life thinking what would get me into Stanford and what would ruin my chances.

Thirdly, these schools are great but what if they aren't for me? What if I'm not a good fit for some of these schools? I was going to do what I wanted and what I liked and what I could do. If I got in, it meant I was a good fit. If not, then there are many other schools where I'll do more than just fine.

I won't delude you into thinking that all these realizations were an act of my self-reflection and deep philosophical thoughts. Because they weren't. I talked to a few people and they made me question my mentality. The fact that I was trying too hard simply meant that I was too desperate and could be smelt from a mile away.

Now, there might be some room for conflict. Reader, you might think I am providing opposition to ambition, that I am criticizing dreams and goals. But reader, I ask you to not get me wrong. I do not propose not dreaming, I do not preach life without ambition, I simply recommend not letting your dreams hold the reins. And sometimes before we realize it, dreams become unhealthy. We constitute our happiness into arriving at a place. But who can guarantee that? Can I guarantee that I'll be happy in Harvard or Yale? Truth is, reader, that I can't. But worrying about not going to a brand school, where I don't even know if I'll be happy, and thus being unhappy, is not a bet I want to wager.

We are way ahead of ages of social hierarchy and brand schools are no more the reserves of the upper class. Brand schools don't promise a successful future; they don't promise happiness. They might get to decide if I'm admitted into their school or not, but they don't get to decide what I am capable of. I'm done running the rat race. I am done trying to outdo people left and right. Because ask yourself, reader, when does this all end? Throughout high school I'll do what I think the college admissions committee wants from me, then throughout college I'll do what graduate school wants from me, then in graduate school I'll do whatever my future employer wants, throughout my job I'll do what a promotion wants of me. So what do I do for myself, reader? What do I do for me? And when do I do it?

chapter 8

Sugar and Spice is What Makes it Nice

The cool breeze rushed past my face causing me to squint. My hair flew in every direction further diminishing my visibility, as I sat by the window of the rented SUV. Although it was dented and scraped, it had its own charm. The gushing noise of the swift wind and the fragrance of the pine and deodar trees had kept me from sleeping. As we drove through the serpentine roads of the mountains, I saw freshly painted milestones and small roadside temples that served as insignificant landmarks. As the car turned, I faced the mountainside. The scene changed and the river that I was gazing at, vanished and I could smell the earth among the overgrown vegetation and the muddy uneven mountain surface. I gazed into space wondering how my life would be if I lived here. Time passed, we went higher into the hills and clouds darkened along with the sound of pattering water droplets. It seemed like ages, but we finally reached what I called my second home, Youreka Camp.

I stepped out of the car, put the rucksack on my back. Feeling experienced and confident, I walked into the camp. Memories flooded back to me. The ground was covered with twigs, dried pine needles, dry leaves and stones. Walking in, I felt like a know-it-all and kept on uttering stuff into my friends' ears. After all, I had been to Youreka six times before. We saw the tents in which we were to spend the next eight days. They were spacious, made of dark coloured fabric and were on wooden stilts about a foot above the ground. The thought of living in them was simply thrilling. There was a shoe rack and a dustbin along with wet clothes hanging on the bamboo rods outside each tent giving it a homely feeling. The flaps of the tents were open just enough to take a peek. There was a single line of tents on both sides and there was a path in between. On the left of the path, was a volleyball court and a black rubber water tank. There was a green fence bordering the camp with climbers, plants growing all over it. There were apricot trees filled with ripe juicy fruits and when you looked at the ground, there was an alarming number of fallen, rotten, overripe apricots, coated in dry mud. If you touched them they were pulpy and compressible. It was quite normal to find instructors and kids on the trees—plucking and throwing down fruit in the hands of hungry children. And on the right of the path, was what I loved most about camp—the beautiful flowing river.

The camp was on the banks of River Tirthan. Across

the river, there was a mountain that seemed to be falling on us. The camp was about two metres above the sea level. There was a small gate in the fence joining a flight of cement stairs that were used for leaving the camp. Though the river was known to be forceful and ferocious, it seemed to be the calmest thing in the world. As the rapids were formed, the Tirthan seemed to be white. Yet you could see the deep greenish-blue shade of the clear flawless water. The river could absorb any problem, your troubles would flow away and before you knew it, they were long lost. I leaned against the fence with my friends at my side. We stood on grey stones as big as a man's fist and stared into the river, which just flowed on tirelessly. The water body was like a piece of play dough as it could be moulded in anyway. Sometimes narrow, other times wide. At times it was slow and calm but then after it rained, it was wild and faster than the wind. The river left me perplexed—how could the same thing take such different forms?

Down the path, was the place where we spent most of our time congregating, gossiping, and most importantly, eating and having fun. It was a permanent structure, unlike the tents, and could hold approximately 100 people. When you are in there, you could hear the slabs of wood creaking, sit on the graffiti painted ledges, criticize the craft made by other groups and admire your own, sing songs in groups which sounded completely uncoordinated and smell the spices in the food which was being freshly made. This place that is ingrained so well in my mind is the KPRD, camp slang for a place where one eats and drinks, laughs and cries. The KPRD looked small from outside though it had huge glass windows, a thatched roof and charts and paintings stuck on its four walls. While there used to be a vibrancy and vitality in the KPRD, the ghanta ghar or clock tower, which was facing the river, was the place for serious discussions, deep thinking and alone time. The ghanta ghar was a huge favourite with the introverts. These small bits of sugar and spice were what made camp a truly exceptional place for me.

The weather fluctuated a lot and it could rain any time without warning. The temperature would fall and the sound of falling raindrops would fill your ears. Whenever I was lucky enough to get the opportunity I would go and sit on the green wooden bench—drinking tea in a steel glass, and watching the river get angry. Raindrops poured down my back and neck, making me shiver. I would absorb heat by tightly holding the glass of tea. Taking a deep breath, I could smell the mixture of wet mud and tea. Often, I would take a huge gulp by mistake and scald the tip of my tongue. The sun would start setting; I would walk away feeling light hearted and blissful, letting my bare feet sink into the damp ground.

chapter 9

Manga to Bollywood

Akari Kagawa. I had read her name outside our dorm room. 'Akari, Akari, Akari…' I had repeated to myself. She was probably Japanese, I thought, maybe Taiwanese or Chinese. No, the name hadn't sounded like it was Chinese. It turned out, she was Japanese. Akari had a small petite build, typical of a Japanese girl. Honestly, I had felt like a hippopotamus in front of her. She had thin, jet-black hair, almond-shaped eyes and rather large glasses on her face. Akari had chosen to study Sustainable Urbanization. When she told me the course she was studying, I had felt sceptical about her. Sustainable Urbanization sounded like those value-based projects I had to do for school. They were thoroughly boring. Honestly, my answer for these projects was always, 'Close the tap while brushing your teeth.' Though I was sure that this would be way more interesting than school projects, school had made environment related issues taste like sour milk.

I began to like Akari. I was fascinated by the Manga comics she read. The most intriguing part about these comics was that they opened not from the right but from the left. Secondly, they were read in a weird square pattern. We spent a lot of time discussing each other's cultures. It is one thing, I feel, to read about a particular culture and quite another to ask people belonging to that culture about whether what you read, is actually true. She was, I think, as excited as I was to get an ethnic insight into another culture. From Ramen noodles, to curries, from chopsticks to eating with fingers, from Japanese to Hindi, from kimonos to saris, our conversations were an entanglement of two different countries from Asia. We also talked about our similarities and how we were distinctly different from the West. I had never liked people asking me, 'Is it true that you go to school on elephants?' and it seemed that she didn't like pre-conceived notions about her country either. I think nobody does.

One day I asked her, 'What about Sustainable Urbanization appeals to you? Isn't it sort of boring?' Her reply surprised me. 'Suman,' she said, in her accent, 'I don't want people in the future to study history and say that their ancestors were selfish and greedy. We think that we're above all animals because we've developed and evolved so much, but I believe we'll be truly advanced the day we can make this last, the day we know we aren't threatening our own existence.' I had thought about what she had said that night. I was struck by the maturity that was contained in her five-feet body.

Akari and I had fun, talking after the lights went out. Sometimes we would eat her Japanese snacks. I never told her but I didn't like the seaweed she used to eat. But I adored her stationery. I had always had a fetish for different coloured pens, mechanical pencils, calligraphy pens, clean paper and just stationery. She was from Japan and I felt that she was blessed by the God of stationery.

At the end of our program she said to me, 'Suman, you've helped me realize how people from different backgrounds can mingle so well. You have never thought that being from different countries means we have a barrier between us. Instead, you've taught me that ethnicity is just a variable, like the different courses we are studying. It doesn't matter but it's fun exchanging different points of views.'

It was a pleasure knowing the Japanese girl who ate seaweed, had great stationery and studied Sustainable Urbanization.

chapter 10

Evanescence

I soon learned that nothing lasts forever—not life, not gifts, not family, not friends. Everything that feels perfect and immune isn't always the way it seems. Things that I never thought could happen, were happening. Whenever I thought I was in total control, things slipped out of my hands like sand. It happened thrice within a span of six months. My mother always told me that whenever you study, revise your lessons the next day and once again the day after, so that it gets ingrained in your mind. That way you never forget it. That summer, it was like God was trying to teach me a lesson, again and again. So that it was embedded in my head and I could never forget it. The lesson of evanescence.

I went for a three-week programme held by Duke University. I made friends, bonds and attachments not only with people but also with my course, my room and just the feeling of being there. Those were the best three weeks of my life. They were filled with ups and downs, but the experience was astounding, I had never felt that sense of belonging before going to Duke. I got emotionally attached and I never really realized that it was over, until it really was. On the last evening, my friends and I sat and cried for three hours. Nothing anybody said or did, stopped us. We were shattered at the thought of never seeing each other again and were broken beyond repair. At least that is what we thought. Those of us who lived in the same city, made promises to meet. Promises to call and keep in touch. It turned out that those words were empty, meaningless. For the first few weeks we talked everyday, cried and missed each other so much that it wounded our hearts. I couldn't believe that the best days of my life were over, finished. I never thought they would ever finish. I never thought that I would stop missing them. I thought even God couldn't do that but time did. I still have days when I miss them so much that I start crying. But I did realize that nothing ever lasts. Someday it finishes and you are left with only memories to cry over, or to cherish. You have pictures to look at and smile, incidents to recall, memories to replay, but it can never replace being there and living the moment. Leaving Duke University was a hard blow for me but something else hit me harder.

My three best friends in school were all I had. Without them, I had no one to go to or talk to. Arzoo, Bhavana and Anita were three names that I always had at the tip of my tongue. It was the same for all of them. We were inseparable. The unconditional love and affection we had for each other got us the envy of fellow classmates. We thought about nothing but us. It wasn't as if we were rude to others or didn't talk to them. We just held polite conversation. We were so closely knit and had no space for an outsider, none at all. A few girls tried coming into our group and being a part of us, but their efforts were fruitless. But then gradually we made a bunch of new friends. We had the same friends but it kind of decreased our closeness. Somehow my friend Anita did not mature like we did or maybe she wasn't comfortable with our new friends. I don't know what exactly the problem was, but she was slowly drifting apart. We still did everything together but it was more like a formality because we were one group. Anita started hanging out with a new girl. I never resented her for that because I knew it was good for her. Finally she was making friends of her own, choosing them on her own and handling problems herself. It was like she didn't need us anymore. She became independent and it was for her betterment, but it didn't change the nagging pain in my heart. I was just so used to sticking up for her, speaking up for her that I just didn't want to believe that she didn't need me anymore. She had always been timid and quiet. Never quite revealing her true self to the class and then all of a sudden, she was on fire, the most happening girl. Maybe it was insecurity from the fact that she started getting the attention I used to get, or maybe the fact that we didn't share the same bond anymore. Whatever it was, it was heart breaking.

She wasn't the only one who had drifted apart. Bhavana, Arzoo and I also had the distance between us growing. I became closer to other friends. They were still my best friends but our bond had become stale. We didn't enjoy each other's company as much as we used to. Arzoo who had been my best friend once upon a time was no longer so. I played basketball every day after school and made the closest friend I ever had, Kanika. Unfortunately we weren't in the same school. Arzoo used to put on mock pretense of being jealous of Kanika and we used to laugh. We tried to take it lightly but we all knew that things had changed. I also got closer to Faiz. He was the only one who had time for me and listened to what I said. He too became my best friend. Bhavana and Arzoo became closer to each other but Arzoo used to be lost in a world of her own, and Bhavana started talking to everyone. She had no specific best friend. It wasn't like we stopped talking or became awkward in each other's company. No, we were still close friends and hung out a lot with our group, which consisted of four more friends. But I knew that we had lost the spark and the love that existed once. Our group of eight didn't move on. I just stopped talking to them. They also started talking less. We started bickering and getting on each other's nerves. Nobody made new friends except Anita. She completely deserted us. We all just didn't talk. Exams were coming up and I had a lot of things on my plate. I became paranoid about my work. I had my love for basketball and the passion started growing. I became obsessed with it. I dreamt, thought, lived, inhaled only basketball. During this period my friend Faiz was probably the only one who understood that I was having a difficult time. I was stressed out. And of course, I had Kanika. The hollow emptiness in my stomach didn't go. I waited but it didn't. I missed them while they were in front of me and even when I was talking to them. I pined for the friendship that used to make me alive. I talked to them about this situation and they partially agreed with me. Laila consoled me and said,

'I know it's not the same Naina, but it will all be alright. God is just checking the strength of our friendship. I love you.'

I tried to take some comfort from what she said but I had no reply. I realized that I should enjoy whatever I have to my heart's content because you never know how long it lives. I learned to cherish every second of my life. I learned nothing lasts, and evaporates at some point. But you have to move on even if it tears you apart. Maybe we all just need space, maybe our friendship will take time, or maybe it will never mend. All I know is that I have to hope and try to move on. What has to happen, will happen.

I once read an article in which a young woman is driving in a car with her father. They get caught in a storm—there is thunder, lightning, heavy rainfall and strong winds. It was indeed a massive frightening storm. All the other cars had stopped on the sides waiting for it to stop. The woman then asks her father if she should also stop the car. Her father refuses and tells her to go on and keep driving. She is puzzled and wonders why her father wants her to drive in this terrible storm when it is so difficult to drive and see what is ahead. Her father gives her no explanation but she continues driving. After an hour, they passed the storm and came out in the sunshine. The disaster was left behind. Her father then noted that those people were still stuck in the middle of the storm, whereas they had left it behind and were now basking in the pleasant warm sunshine. He told her to go on with life no matter what obstacle came, because that's the way you can ever gain happiness. Otherwise you will just be stuck in it—depressed, waiting for it to go away. Which won't happen.

I understood what it meant and knew it theoretically, but I guess you never know what it really means until you experience it. I plan to go on and wait with anxiety for that warmth and happiness to come because I have faith. It may not come the way I want it to, I may never share that bond with them again because nothing lives forever except the earth and the moon. But I know something will replace the aching hollowness in my stomach, and let me breathe again.

chapter 11

Not Belonging in the Game

Anita Mahindra is a friend of mine who is slightly bitter that we, her friends, leave her and go to play basketball. She is feeling out of place and is trying her best to not care about it, but it's hurting her inside.

Bitter, resentful, feeling that you don't belong.

Not Belonging in the Game
PE is one period my friends are crazy about. Jumping, running, sweating in the sun, screaming—they love it, every bit about PE. I too like it a lot but I guess I don't die for the games period like my friends do. I suppose they like it because they play their favorite game, basketball. It's not that I hate basketball, don't get me wrong, I just don't like playing with them. They don't bother even passing the ball to us until they are completely stuck. By us, I mean people who just stand and do nothing but mess up when the ball

comes to our hands. I do feel neglected, I mean can't we play something more common? They haven't stopped me from playing anything else, but it is not the same without them. I feel as if I don't belong. It's not only about basketball, they crack jokes that I don't understand and exchange high fives and I just stare at their face. Anyway, I sit on the benches, it's more fun. I know Naina and Bhavana kind of feel guilty that I don't play but there is nothing much I can do. I want to show them that I can keep myself busy and don't necessarily depend on them. So like always, I walked to the sports complex with other girls because when the bell rings for PE, my friends forget about me and rush to the basketball court. They decided to play girls versus boys and chose all the dominant players. Obviously, the game is all about winning and having the best players and not about including everyone and having a great time. Bhavana asked me if I wanted to play and I declined the offer. I prefer sitting on the side and talking to other girls who don't like playing basketball and irritating Sahil, not bullying just teasing. The girls started the game and Naina passed to Arzoo who dribbled and took the ball to the other side and passed to Bhavana who then gave it to Naina, who attempted shooting as usual, the ball spun thrice around the ring in slow motion creating suspense and then tipped outside into the guys' hands. The girls groaned and then shot off to the other side for defence. Yeah basically, the ball comes to only the three of them. I was having fun goofing around. We were sitting on the bleachers under the blazing sun when Naina suddenly came to us grumbling that none of her shoots were going in and sat and put her head in my lap. I consoled the poor girl. She complained more about something called a lay up. I feel so out of place. If I tell her I don't know what a lay up is, she'll probably freak out. Arzoo comes and tells me to lay off Sahil and asks Naina to come back into the game. God, why do they behave as if they can't play without her? She says she doesn't feel like playing and Arzoo too comes and sits by us. Arzoo and Naina keep on shouting stuff to their teammates giving advice and encouraging them, I wonder if they are so interested, why don't they go and play themselves. Well just as I was thinking about this, both of them jumped and ran into the game simultaneously. God only knows what happened. I feel that I am not one of them and there is no place for me in their group. Sahil got sick of us bothering him and went to the other side of the court, and obviously we followed him. We were not going to let him go so easily. Laughing and giggling, we went after him. The people playing basketball looked to see what was happening and exchanged knowing looks and grinned. It was a daily ritual of girls teasing Sahil and him retorting. Irritating him is my favourite hobby. He is such a fun target. After a while the bell rang. Sweating and worn out, all my friends started heading back towards the class. They were in deep discussion about what went wrong, who's good at defence, who shoots well, and how they need taller players in their team. And it was typical of me to not have any conversation to make. They are absolutely obsessed with basketball; they'll do anything for it. I mean come on, it's just a game and they argue so much about it. The guys had won, which was quite a shock because they usually loose by 16-2, or something like that. I am in deep thought about how out of place I am while they are arguing somewhere in the background.

chapter 12

Time to Turn the Page

Laughter roared in my ears, and I looked across the room. Faiz Dixit was joking around with a couple of his friends. Our eyes met for a second and we both looked away. His previously smiling expression had now turned grim. I sighed deeply. There was a twinge of regret, deep down inside me, for the silent treatment that we were giving each other. I couldn't help but remember how things used to be, which brought memories flooding back. It was something I didn't want to relive, but I was at peace with my past now.

It all started in 6th grade. I came into middle school, where there were new people, new teachers and some newfound freedom. I wasn't ready for change, and neither were my three best friends. So it was Laila, Arzoo, Inayat and me. It was us against the world. So while people around us were changing and getting into what they thought was grown-up stuff, we were content by ourselves. During this time one of my childhood friends Kabir was going with the flow. While I had my mates, he didn't have any friends, so he had to find his way through. He eventually made friends, but I didn't really like them. They didn't take academics seriously, thought too much of themselves and I guess, they just had this vibe about them that made me uneasy. I didn't approve of them but it wasn't my place to interfere, so I didn't. I became the SOTM, which stands for Student of the Month. This basically meant that I was the class prefect for a month. During that time, an incident took place which involved Faiz, Kabir and a couple of their friends getting into trouble.

I remember telling him, 'They're not good for you Kabir, and I don't think you should hang out with them.'

Had he listened, I would have been at a very different point in life. I hated Faiz, but I had my own life to live and couldn't be bothered with his.

Plus life was going absolutely great for me. I had everything—great friends, good grades, a happy family and till then a drama free life. I was constantly laughing, joking around and was naïve. I thought the world was full of sweet-eyed angels. Little did I know.

At the end of sixth grade, I don't know how or why, Kabir and I began talking again. Largely the whole year had gone by without us interacting, but this was the first step to a friendship that would go a long way. I didn't know this at that time. I was just waiting to see what would happen.

As Kabir and I became better friends, our friends had to interact with each other's friends too. Slowly, I became okay with Faiz's presence. Even though my gut was against him, I eventually started talking to him. I kind of accepted the fact that he was Kabir's friend. Now like any typical story all of us became friends. By all of us I mean Laila, Inayat, Arzoo, Kabir, Faiz, Ranbir, Jai and I.

Our friendship was a gradual process, from occasional formal conversations to frequent casual exchanges of words to being one inseparable group. It was unsaid between us but we knew that we had each other's backs. It was not about 'me' anymore but about 'us.' We went to the same parties, sat next to each other in school, had our set of inside jokes and more than anything, we knew everything about each other. That was the best part about our group; we never hid anything from each other. It was a fairytale.

I won't say everything was perfect because it wasn't. We had our share of problems. Moreover, it was like living inside a soap opera. We were full of drama. We dealt with insecurities, not having enough time for each other, taking a joke too seriously and just regular stupid fights almost on a daily basis. But when we were together as one, it was magical. At the end of the day, we were still there for each other.

There came a point, when things turned bad, really bad. It was the beginning of 9th grade. I used to sit with Faiz and Kabir. We were really close, but lately both of them had started bickering a lot. I couldn't help but notice constant jabs they took at each other. I tried to ignore it or behave as if it was normal but somehow I always got stuck in the middle. They used to ask me who was right and who was wrong, but I thought they were both really immature to be fighting over petty issues. I mean they were best friends. I tried to be fair and take both their sides equally but I guess I was wrong. According to Faiz, I always talked to Kabir and preferred him. I didn't know what to do. Whenever I was to him, he told me I didn't have to talk to him because I had to or because he would feel bad otherwise. He never came to talk to me either; it was I who always went to him. I don't know what went wrong. I mean where were the days when we used to be best friends. Every time something funny or familiar happened, we used to exchange glances and laugh, we used to talk for so long at the end of the day even after all the buses would leave and then finally decide it was late and we should go home. He told me everything and so did I. We used to poke fun at Kabir together and joke at his expense. But it was gone. All of it. Just because he had this idea in his head that I didn't care about him. It was just sad at first but then slowly it didn't just remain sad, it turned nasty. Faiz had given me no explanation as to why he was ignoring me. He just stopped talking to me one fine day. I guess he told Ranbir and Jai something that turned them against me too. Both of them didn't just ignore me, they got into a fight with me. Ranbir and I shouted at each other, with hair in my face and fury boiling inside me and both our faces flushed with anger, our fight wasn't a very pleasant scene. We both said things that hit each other's weakest nerves. Times were turning bad for me; with everyone against me, I was alone. I pushed away the people who wanted to be with me. I turned them away. I gave curt replies on the phone, sat away from everyone at school, starting missing school frequently. I had dark circles, I snapped at everyone and my friends started to worry. I wanted to get away from this. What's wrong with my life, was my constant question. This continued for three months. Fortunately for me, the summer vacation started. It was an opportunity to break away.

I had a long time to think about this during the summer. I thought how could someone who I used to be such good friends with, stop caring overnight. I contemplated whether there was some other reason for his refraining. He never told me the reason. He just said that I had changed. I don't know what that meant. He moved on. Clearly, he couldn't care less. While my wounds were visible to the world, his indifference was evident as well. I mean this was a phase where I was split into two. Part of me wanted to go and sort everything out, the part that missed them. But another part was shouting at me and asking me to never get so close to someone again, especially not them. It was telling me not to stray too far from the sidewalk.

One day I was sitting on the cream colored couch, curling up with my golden Labrador, eating cookie dough ice cream and watching chick flicks. Then it hit me. If I just eliminated them from my life, everything is perfect. I have four amazing friends and just because it didn't work out with Jai, Ranbir and Faiz, didn't mean everyone was going to hurt me. I was punishing myself by pushing Laila, Arzoo, Inayat and Kabir away. I was topping my class, I had family support, I was in the basketball team and I had dreams. Dreams that I wanted to fulfill. I realized that some things are just not worth it. If Faiz, Ranbir and Jai hated me, it was fine with me. I wasn't going to lose any more sleep over them, as it is I had wasted enough. Bob Marley once said, 'The truth is, everyone is going to hurt you. You just got to find the ones worth suffering for.' But the thing is, before you're hurt you think the person is worth it, but after it's over, you think that person was never worth it and you made a mistake. After school began, I learnt that he had really been talking behind my back and had said a lot of bad stuff. I was shocked. I mean I knew we weren't talking but I didn't know he hated me that much. It was hard but I realized I didn't want to be friends with him again. I made up with Ranbir and Jai, but I kept my distance. I had learnt one thing—sometimes you have to let go. Just leave everything, all the pointless drama in life and all the negativity that's drowning you. And once you move on, it's like you can breathe again. You're free. I felt like I could do anything, I didn't have to live up to anyone's expectations, I didn't have to sit with particular people. My life was my own to live. I had friends whom I loved but I was never going to let anyone else affect me anymore. My life was my own to control. Life was about pursuing my passions, dreaming and following my goals. Somewhere along the line, I had given up on my dreams like I had on my friends. I had fallen badly but I had the strength to get up and I just had to walk in the right direction. I had been hurt, alone and upset but Faiz had taught me it was time to turn the page.

I turned my head to look at him again. Now I smile. I smile with regret because it wasn't the way I wanted it to end. I smile with relief that it's over and I don't have to go through it again. I smile sadly because I remember the fun times we had. I smile proudly because I know that I got up even when I had fallen so badly. I smile through my tears, the smile that tells everyone who I am. A girl who just realized what life was worth living for.

Part II

chapter 13

My Struggle with Atheism

Is man merely a mistake of God?
Or God merely a mistake of man?

—FREIDRICH NIETZSCHE

It was during the summer vacations of 2008. My Gigi and Nana had come to spend the day. My mom's sisters and my cousins were visiting as well. I always loved family get-togethers. Firstly, they always consisted of bucket loads of food; every meal was a feast. We were a family raised and brought up in Delhi. Food was an essential part of every activity. We were the kind of family that centered gatherings specifically around food. Ordering food or deciding where to go for a meal, was always a big decision. One we all took very seriously. No one in my family jokes about food; it's an unwritten rule.

The second reason for my love, was that we were an affectionate and close-knit family. Most of us were armed with a good sense of humour—it comes with the food—and I'd be doubling over for a majority of the time. The third reason was that I, like any other child, loved to hear adults talk. I was always extremely fascinated with whatever conversation the adults of the family seemed to be having. I always had my two cents to add, even if no one listened to me. It mostly ended in everyone laughing me off. But I was resilient. Often I'd go back to school and quote my family to my friends in an attempt to sound smart and grown up. It worked. They fed my ego well as they lapped up every word I said. It's safe enough to say I was an overconfident kid who thought she was better than other people her age. I loved listening to adult conversation and felt important when they talked to me. So when my grandmother first introduced me to Buddhism, I was obviously intrigued. She too, I suppose, took advantage of my childhood zeal. I hung on to every word she said, feeling like I'd been endowed with a crucial, and more importantly, adult task.

After lunch everyone went to their respective rooms to take their afternoon nap. Sleep was important to our family, as well. I, on the other hand, was a hyperactive kid who hated nap time. I didn't understand why they'd bother sleeping when they could play Monopoly instead. Monopoly, might I add, is the game of the Gods. Quite modestly speaking, I'm the Monopoly Queen.

'Izar, come here, I'm going to teach you something new today,' Gigi said in that soft yet firm voice of hers, beckoning me onto her lap.

'Okay! What?' I perked up. And hoisted myself up on her lap.

My grandmother was a no nonsense woman. She was a reasonably practical lady, especially for someone of that day and age. She herself had been introduced to Buddhism a few years back and had taken to it almost immediately. She sat me down in our terrace garden and explained to me this concept of chanting in Buddhism. It was a simple philosophy really. If you recite something enough number of times, you send out vibrations of what you want into the universe. And the universe, duty bound, has to make it happen. Of course this had to be accompanied by all necessary action on your part. But if you followed the rules, success was yours. She told me I could have anything I wanted if I chanted. For me this was like a bottomless jar of genie wishes. I had my doubts; it seemed too good to be true. But I suppose it's not difficult to convince a child that this kind of sorcery actually exists. No wonder most of the population believes in God. The believers get to them when they're young.

'Nam-myoho-renge-kyo' was the magic mantra. Carefully, in her gentle yet firm demeanour, she guided me through the steps. I was to carry them out every day. Of course that never happened. I had a patience deficiency. Too bad it didn't show up in the blood test.

Law abiding little child that I was, I lacked the outright defiance to refuse to chant when Gigi called me to join her.

She was convinced this worked. She was a believer and you can't argue with religious people. If you could, there would be no religious people. I totally quoted from *House* here and tried to take the credit for it. Anyway to be honest, I had no reason to not believe her. Moreover, my respect for her would not allow me to refuse her request that I chant with her.

I remember using this concept in my life when I really needed it. Chanting myself to sleep when my parents used to fight, hurriedly muttering the words when I really wanted to convince my mother to buy me something or as a last resort, chanting when I didn't study for a test, in hope that the Buddhists will come to my rescue. Didn't work. Very early in life I realized how human beings function. We pray when we want something. We pray because we're selfish and scared. I do not condemn those who do. I won't even say they're delusional. I'll just say religion didn't work out for me. Everything that I believed in, my entire moral system rejected the idea of prayer. Praying is weak and like I said, a last resort.

The 'believers' around me, very often do not even realize how often they use the word God. I have over the years become so hyperaware of the word, that every time someone uses it my ears cock like that of a dog's. I am so conscious of the abundance in which this word is used that sometimes I ask myself, 'Do people actually believe that heavily in God?'

God has given you this, God has given you that.

He's God-gifted.

God is always watching. That's like religion's version of Big Brother is watching. And let me remind you that *1984* was a dystopian novel.

God didn't want that for you.

God will protect you.

Thank you God for everything you've done for me.

I will not pretend to come across as extremely tolerant for I am not. I do have moments of extreme frustration when I see people acting 'irrationally' according to me. Although I was not born into a particularly religious household my parents did believe in a God and often referred to him/her. But then believing in God does not mean being religious. My parents would use phrases like 'God has gifted you with so and so...' or 'God is watching what you're doing'. Later I realized these phrases were mere translations of 'You've been lucky' and 'Remember what goes around comes around'. As a child I would often pray to an omnipotent being, I would pray in a temple or a church, I would even fear God. When my parents used to go out at night, and I feared Wee Willy Winky would take me away, I used to fall asleep holding a small statue of God. But growing up, I began to question this unyielding belief that everyone around me had. In someone or something that none of them have seen or heard of.

However open-minded society might be becoming, however accepting it might be, the notion that God does not exist is quite absurd and more than shocking, it's unimaginable. Sometimes I feel that when I tell someone that I don't believe in God it kind of goes over their head as if what I've said is beyond the realm of human comprehension.

Sometimes I struggle to comprehend why is it that 99 per cent of the human population believes in a higher power or God. What is it about this faith that calls out to so many people without a shred of evidence?

Rigid mindsets have gradually evolved with each age, each generation brining its own set of evils. Society has learned to recognize women as equal to men, to accept a working woman, different faiths have accepted divorce, or alcohol, and it has come to slowly accept even homosexuality, cross dressing, abortion, trans-genderism. These were all things that were seen as 'wrong' once upon a time. It happened, but it was frowned upon. However, the same is not the case with being a non-believer. People don't get outraged when they hear me say that I don't believe in God; they simply don't believe me. Moreover, they give me funny looks. When will people realize atheism is not equal to Satanism? We're not a cult. Don't treat us like one.

Being an atheist becomes controversial when people start accusing you of disregarding people's beliefs. But what people often forget is that atheism is a belief too. Praying goes against the beliefs of an atheist. If an atheist stands up and says, 'There is no God' then atheism gets tagged as being a set of intolerant non-believers. But that is not true. In fact, most atheists walk on eggshells because they have to be careful not to hurt anyone's religious or spiritual sentiments. But the matter of fact is that religious people are way less tolerant of atheists and non-believers. Why do they get a right to be sensitive? When they can outright tell me that my belief is wrong, is it really me being insensitive? Is it really me being intolerant?

I have always liked playing the devil's advocate. My inherent need to question authority perhaps led me to doubt this massive notion around which majority of people seemed to centre their lives. If people want to believe in God, I respect that. But what I am vehemently opposed to, is teaching children to believe in God. From a young age, all of us are brainwashed. We read and hear about God everywhere as though He were indeed real. Why can't we give them an opportunity to come to their own belief without telling them what to actually believe in?

When little kids feel scared, parents tell them that God will protect them. They tell them to not lie because God is always watching and knows the truth. He will punish those who do wrong. This is the easy way out. But I do understand the contradiction in my own suggestion. Parents will always impose their value system on their children. If they truly believe in God, then that is what they will teach their children. They can't tell them that 'Maybe God exits. Maybe he doesn't. You just have to figure it out for yourself,' if they themselves are convinced that God exists. Because the second you start questioning your own beliefs, is the second they cease to be your absolute beliefs.

I feel the same goes for a lot of other beliefs. Instead of telling our little girls that they'll get husbands or our boys to find a wife, if we simply told them to find a partner, girl or boy, the world would be more open to homosexuality. Children aren't born with beliefs. And we shouldn't teach them what to believe. We need to teach them how to question. Brainwashing will never lead to development, because before we can develop the world, we need to develop human thought.

I love Gigi. But I don't believe in Buddhism. This isn't disrespect for her or for Buddhism. This is simply my belief. A belief that I believe is right. There is no God. You can sue me for saying that, but what would God say?

chapter 14

The Indian Dream

*It's easier to fool people than
to convince them they've been fooled.*

—MARK TWAIN

My classmate and friend, Elina Pandey wants to be an engineer. Pooja Arora wants to be a doctor. Sahil Goel wants to be a computer scientist. They are 100 per cent sure about what they want to be. Am I the only 'bright student' in my class who is not sure about studying science in 11th grade? Somehow nobody around me says, 'I am positive I want to be a journalist, or a lawyer, or an investment banker.' But I always hear 'I want to be a doctor', 'I want to be an engineer' or 'I want to pursue information technology as a career'. This mindset has led to the confinement of social sciences and humanities. Furthermore, many young people are steered into a life they would not have otherwise chosen. India has to realize the harmful effects of idolizing and enforcing science on its new generation of students. Post-independence, India's obsession with studying science and scientific research is unhealthy and constraining. It is the next social prejudice that India has to do away with.

Thousands of students take the entrance exams. But we all know, that there are only a few who are actually going to make it. It is practically pre-decided. Some people take the exams for the sake of it, knowing that they don't know anything. Some take them after spending a considerable amount of time preparing, thinking that they might get in. But the truth is, they need a miracle to actually clear the exam. Then there are those, who are brilliant, hard working, self-motivated, they have what my mother calls the 'killer instinct.' They walk in knowing that they have done everything required, they crack the exam, discover the secret recipe. But only, it isn't a secret. They have not only studied for the exam but have studied the exam itself.

The foundations of Indian education are exams similar to the National Talent Search Examination. If you clear the test, you get a scholarship till PhD level. But more than the scholarship it is the name that is more valuable, NTSE. Being an NTSE scholar means a remarkable addition to the resumé. It's probably what makes a good CV, an exceptional CV.

Now you might think, 'Why is this exam such a big deal?' In India there are two things that make an exam prestigious. The first is the sheer number of people taking it. The number of people taking the exam is proportional to the level of importance of the exam. And obviously as the exam becomes more important, more people want to take it. The second factor is how much syllabus one has to cover, how many hours one has to put in. Now as the number of hours rise, the prestige of the exam increases. 'Who can put in how many hours?' seems to become the question. One would assume that the increased number of hours needed to prepare would scare a lot of kids and parents. But no, not us Indians. Even if we don't intend on preparing sufficiently, we still take the exam. We question, 'What's the harm in taking it?' while secretly hoping that clearing the exam will mean one more addition to our resumé.

But this exam is the very essence of what it means to be a typical student growing up in India. Hard work is the lesson we learn before the alphabet. Competition is the reality we accept before God. Focused is what we are, before being Indian.

So not surprisingly, all Indians dream about getting into the most famous, the most respected, and the most competitive engineering institute—IIT.

The IITs—Indian Institutes of Technology—are the most celebrated engineering institutes of India. Launched in 1950, the IITs have served as a ticket to success in people's careers. The IITs were in fact given the status 'Institutes of National Importance' by the government. There exists only one way of getting into this premier institute, which is clearing the IIT Joint Entrance Exam (IIT JEE). You write the exam and then you are ranked. Only the top rankers get the subject and location (city) of their choice. Now if you are thinking that the JEE is your average entrance exam, that's where you are mistaken. It is a bigger deal than the SAT, it is as big, if not bigger, than the Bar Exam. Preparing for the IIT is a two-year project at the very least.

An average applicant puts in 40-50 hours a week of self-study (based on my observation and discussion with peers who are preparing for IIT), not including school and coaching classes. Include those, an IIT aspirant studies for 100-110 hours a week. Most of them sleep a maximum of seven hours a day. The healthy requirement of the body is eight hours a night for adults. So IIT applicants have little time left every day for anything else, which includes taking a bath, meals, chores, personal work and the rest to relax a bit. This seems laborious, almost torturous, in front of the French 35-hour work-week.

Nearly five lakh Indian students take the JEE every year. That is half a million. And how many clear it? Ten thousand. If it still hasn't sunk in, I'll repeat. One in fifty make it to the end. That means IIT has a 2 per cent acceptance rate. So look around you, the fifty people you see surrounding you, only one of you will make it. Look at the five hundred people surrounding you, only one of you will make it to the top one thousand. And if you want to study Computer Science or Electrical Engineering, you'll have to beat those

500 kids. About 1 per cent of college basketball players make it to the NBA, and only 0.8 per cent people taking the JEE get a subject of their choice. And NBA is the far-fetched dream.

Some might see beauty in the way an underdog rises to the top, after years of labouring and working for something. I respect hard work. I respect determination. I respect ambition. But I cannot respect a system that encourages children to make an exam the focus of their life. I cannot admire those lives. I can only pity. How can a parent tell their child to breathe only the stale air of the room they are going to be locked up in, studying? They are told that this will guarantee them a secure future. This is 'ideal' Indian life. This is the 'Indian Dream'.

A typical conversation on a child's career options can go like this:

'Do you like Physics? Oh you must like Math then? No? You must want to pursue Medicine? So what are you doing after school?'

'Uncle, I don't really like Math and Physics.'

'So what are you aiming at?'

'IIT'

'But you just said you don't enjoy Math and Physics!'

'That's completely irrelevant. Mummy and Papa say IIT is my only shot.'

'Why? Aren't there other options?'

'I score high marks in school, it'll be a waste if I don't

study engineering.'

Now stop. We have reached the crux of the argument. This is pivotal to understanding the Indian psyche.

Being smart in school equals taking science as a subject in high school. Taking science equals pursuing a career in engineering or medicine. Now, who decided that science required a higher IQ? When we as regular people utter statements like the above, we do not realize the weight and enormity of what we are speaking. When we say, 'I am smart, therefore I should become an engineer or a doctor,' we immediately lower the standard of every other profession. The underlying meaning immediately gets highlighted. But it is not that science is tougher, it is that we have dumbed the level of humanities in our country. We have made humanities a subject easier than it is, we have taken the easy route. And how can things be compared when one is at its finest glory and the other a cowering second option? Engineering and medicine are at the top of this caste hierarchy, and caste elimination has been our battle for years.

The IITs were developed with the hope of creating some of the finest engineers in the world. When we got independence, Jawaharlal Nehru, Independent India's first prime minister, saw technology as the lifeboat that would guide India towards self-reliance. India stood a stark contrast to Britain, when it came to technological development. The British, after the Industrial Revolution, had progressed a lot while India still remained distant from technology. The

British machine-made goods, trains and ships, their advanced ammunition, made Indian goods seem primitive. Nehru, being a pioneer of scientific education, had greatly promoted the development of the IITs. Who knew Nehru's ideology on scientific education would be mimicked in the mind of every Indian parent? Who knew that engineering and medicine would be seen as the only respectable professions? Who knew India would become a land of mass-produced engineers? Who knew that, like same-caste marriage, IIT too would become a part of the Indian mindset? Is the alignment of our moral compass correct, if we force engineering on the children of this country? Or should I say, is our thinking correct if we see science as a godly subject and other subjects as mediocre?

And what kind of engineers is this obsession with science producing for India? Does the maddening preparation for IIT JEE expand the children's knowledge, does it develop their thinking? It does not and that is the problem. The goal of the IITs is to admit the brightest kids of the country, who are also the most sincere. But the loophole in the whole concept of JEE is bigger than the hole in the ozone layer. The test does not see who is the brightest, it just sees who is the most prepared, not for IIT, but for the JEE.

IIT, Indian Institute of Technology—creating engineers who don't like engineering since the 1950s. The IIT graduate is celebrated. The degree is prized above the child. A symbol of prestige. To me, it is a symbol of a handcuffed journey through which students are dragged on the ground. And then, they smile and say, 'I have a great life.'

Now let's talk about those who don't get in. Those who have the misfortune of wasting years studying for something they don't like. They don't even get to live the joys and pleasures of the Indian Dream. What happens to them? First, they try again. Eventually hopes are shattered and the Indian Dream comes to screeching halt. Then they stop. And they think.

I'm not saying there aren't people who are passionate about engineering who apply to IIT. Because there are. But the sheer number of people who don't have a knack for engineering, who don't want to be doctors but are trying to make themselves happy by going by what society has termed successful is alarming. Sometimes, I think the line between wanting to be an engineer and just wanting the world to see you as an engineer gets smudged. This is a joke. Only in the end, I don't see anyone laughing. A contradiction arises. It is clichéd to do what society wants you to do. And now when everyone is preaching that you follow your heart, that's become clichéd too. But I'll say there is a difference. Disney movies show that you should follow your dream. But dreaming is not always as dramatic as becoming a glamorous pop star with bestselling albums from a quiet, five-feet girl, who lives in a town no one has heard of. No, that is not what I am talking about. But just studying something you like? That's not as far-fetched as Cinderella, is it?

Where this notion about science arises from, I understand. Coming from a country lagging behind in technology, I can understand this need for engineers. I also understand the parents' reasoning for wanting their children to study science. They feel there is job security, a certain standard and respect guaranteed. But we're talking about old times. Our fledgling country was in a dire situation and it seemed there weren't too many 'safe' career options. But ideas have developed, people have become wealthier and professions have expanded. Today, creativity, innovation, and passion have a place. Times have changed, and the clock waits to strike a new ideology. Saying one subject is better than another is like saying one colour is better than another. We can't say purple is better than blue, we can only say we prefer it. Similarly, you can't say physics is better than economics. Because tell me what is the metre by which you're measuring? What's the benchmark? How can you paint a picture with only one colour? How can you draw with only one line?

We need to give the children of this country a choice. We need to be fair and give social sciences and humanities the glory it deserves. We need to show our children that if they decide to study history, they won't be deemed stupid. We need to teach better. We need to teach our children so they become well educated and learned people, not so they can obtain a degree. We need to teach our subjects, in their raw and pristine form. Adulterated books and monotonous education systems need to be done away with. As a country we need to increase the quality of our education by more than just a notch. We need to give everyone the freedom of attaining salvation through knowledge. Let it be known that the heart is free to wander the streets of education.

chapter 15

Irony of Privacy

*Privacy on the internet?
That's an oxymoron.*
—CATHERINE BUTLER

How many people speed despite knowing that if you're lucky, it is just a ticket and if luck decides it's not on your side that particular day, then folks, it's death. Logically one would think it's considerably unwise to speed, bearing in mind what the possible outcome is. Heaven knows, I'm screeching at whoever's driving the car when I'm getting late for school. But then in my case, the wrath of my principal is worse than death. Yet CNN reports, 'Forty percent admit to driving more than 20 miles per hour over the speed limit.' Why? Because everybody thinks that it is just unlikely that they will meet with an accident. It is turning a blind eye to the point of stupidity. Well, the problem is not very different when you come to internet. People don't take internet security seriously because they think it is just too unlikely that they are going to be victimized. This is why most people don't think even once before they put something on the internet. They don't realize how every step they take online is reflected offline. I previously had a blog on which I used to post mostly philosophical quotes, self-written paragraphs, inspirational sayings and pictures. It was a place where I thought I connected with people, even though I had no followers, because I assumed that no one I knew in real life was reading my blog. However, one day, a friend of mine mentioned that he had read something on my blog. I was shocked at the prospect of him reading posts into which I had poured my heart. Several other people too later mentioned reading my blog, and a couple of my friends laughed at me, telling me I was so serious about life. That is when I realized that nothing could be hidden on the internet. Everything that reaches the net can be accessed, no matter how much one tries to hide it. Granted I didn't really try to hide my blog, anyone who looked me up would've found it. But the point was that the internet wasn't as different a world as I'd thought it to be. With technology taking over, people treating online privacy issues as trivial and the vastness of the internet, cybercrime, privacy violation and online harassment are the inevitable social evils of the coming years.

The internet has become the new platform for all activities, and it is only natural that society will have a whole set of problems related to it. The only reason why these problems are so serious and alarming is because no one seems to take them seriously. 'Oh the internet, what could go wrong?' Ask those who have committed suicide due to cyber bullying, or those whose intimate pictures have been leaked all over the net, or that one person who didn't get a job because his prospective employer saw that one tweet he made seven years ago. Hmm, I really wonder what could go wrong! The internet sure is useful, but we have to tread with caution. Dismissing its potential threat is being really naïve or dumb. Everybody uses a knife to cut, in fact it's one of the most essential tools of kitchen, but that doesn't mean we don't use it carefully. What would happen if we used it carelessly? A lot of bandages, stitches, visits to the emergency room, and so on. The same is with the internet, use it but don't forget the damage it is capable of.

Privacy on the internet is a term which has become more like a ritual. It isn't taken seriously. Everybody will update their privacy settings on Facebook, but what use is that when people accept friend requests from strangers, just so the friends count goes higher. I've done it. Or when suddenly someone's ex best friend decides that these pictures could look better photoshopped or in their boss's office. What people don't understand is that the offline and online world do not work the same way. What is said and done offline is only written in pencil, easy erasable, but online, everything is written in permanent marker. It sets records that can be viewed by anybody, anytime. Moreover, what happens offline is limited to a small number of people, and one must rely on word of mouth for it to spread. What happens between two people sitting in the doctor's waiting room is witnessed only by them and perhaps a very meddlesome person sitting next to them. Whereas if someone is following somebody around with a video camera, scribbling notes and staring at that person, it would be kind of obvious what the person is trying to do. Stalking is just a tad bit more difficult in the real world.

What makes the internet so daunting is the absolute lack of awareness that accompanies it. Nobody knows if he or she is being watched or not, or by whom. Also on the internet, it doesn't take time for something to go viral. Once leaked, a piece of very disturbing news could spread faster than spilled milk; you try to control it from one side with a paper napkin and it starts dripping from the other end. Putting information about oneself on the internet is like going around giving random people the key to one's safe, without knowing what one is doing.

People upload information about themselves online, oblivious to who is viewing it and how it is being used against them. Moreover, due to factors such as feeble privacy settings, hackers and the desire of people to misuse power, the internet and social media are becoming incapable of 'protecting' privacy. Privacy invasion can lead to many things. First, people simply do not want strangers stalking them or observing them, however harmless they might be. However, a point that can be argued here is that if people are uploading information about themselves, they do not have the right to stop anyone from using, viewing and absorbing that information. But ask this, if someone leaves her purse on the table, is it all right for someone else to come and pocket it? Privacy isn't a person's obligation to hide secrets, but another person's moral responsibility to leave other people alone. While some may agree or disagree with that, the fact remains that a rectitudinous character will not cross over another person's boundaries of privacy till invited. However, being realistic and keeping in mind that quite a few people do not, in fact, care about being moral, it must be accepted that privacy issues are going to arise. There is going to be a threat to privacy.

The ironical part is that people are so fidgety when it comes to privacy; they are constantly demanding their rights to discretion, yet openly and willingly making their lives public. Teenagers want their parents to give them their 'space' and 'privacy', while they go and make it known to world what they like, what they don't like, who they're dating and what they're doing every single moment of their lives. How contradictory is that? But what most people consider unimportant and innocuous can turn into an ugly situation, which can cause emotional, psychological and sometimes even physical harm. Stalking is one of the effects of personal lives being displayed publicly online. Some stalkers may be harmless, but others can be dangerous. Imagine if the stalker started sending death threats to the victim, or got the person's address and physically started stalking that person. Another problem that arises due to this internet privacy issue is that it has given birth to another form of bullying, cyber bullying—something that society could have done without, considering bullying already happens on a large scale. Bullying used to be limited to the school playground but has advanced onto endless grounds where everyone looks the same. What makes cyber bullying even more malignant, is that it is harder to put an end to it than to the forms of bullying that take place offline. It is difficult to know who is bullying the person, whether through emails, rude posts or texts, if the bully wishes to keep his or her identity anonymous.

Also one of the major problems that is linked to privacy violation, is that people are under careful surveillance by the government. The National Security Administration (NSA) is keeping track of anyone it considers suspicious, without the person's consent. They tap into phone calls, hack into Facebook and email accounts, and keep track of all activities on the internet. Right or wrong is a different question; the truth is, people don't have much of a choice. But if people want to minimize the possibilities of this situation, they will avoid revealing anything they don't want on the front page of the newspaper. On the internet the magnitude of opportunity for breaching privacy, is exponential, unlike any other social medium. This era of socializing is a labyrinth—extremely large, dangerous and easy to get lost in. You can't trace something after it's out there.

The effects of revealing information on the internet are countless. Thus, people should be careful of what they post, keeping in mind that that information could quite easily be available to the world. Companies such as Google and Facebook have weak privacy settings, which can be hacked without complicated resources. Not only that, today we are using the term 'privacy' too casually. People need to remember that if they don't keep their speed in check they might be the next ones to meet an accident, because it can happen to anyone. The dictionary meaning of privacy is 'being free from observation or surveillance', but it has turned into hiding general information and wanting one's own 'space.' But that is like keeping the blinds down but leaving the web cam on. What about the fact that our lives are practically displayed for the world to see? Doesn't that question privacy in its purest form? I have realized that my blog is accessible not only to my friends and family, who might at most judge me, but also to all those people who for some reason might want to harm me. I may not be able to prevent someone else from harming me, but I can control what I post and what information I reveal. If I didn't want people who knew me to read my blog, I should have used a pseudonym. Because the internet can only protect what it doesn't know.

chapter 16

What Would Stalin Say

*The end may justify the means,
as long as there is something to justify the end.*
—LEON TROTSKY

Moral righteousness. I think I try to compensate for my lack of religious beliefs by being extra involved in questions of morality. I got interested in philosophy sometime ago.

Hmm. So let's start with a hypothetical situation. Now, imagine that you are a doctor and you have six patients with you, each one in a critical situation. Five of these patients need immediate organ transplants. They're all different organs of course. And the sixth patient has a fifty-fifty chance of surviving. Now you as a doctor know that you could use the sixth patient as an organ donor and save all the other five lives. What do you do? Here it's a simple comparison, right? One life versus five lives? The more logical part of us says we should save the five lives. After all it is for the 'greater good' but the more morally conscientious part of us asks the question, 'Can we really compare lives?' and 'Who are we to decide who lives and who dies?'

These ethical conundrums puzzled me for a significant amount of time. By no means did I reach any solution that was satisfactory. I mean how is it possible to even answer something like this?

And it is true. What authority do we have to make a decision about who gets to live and who doesn't? That sixth person had rights. That person had the right to live, to make the decision whether she wanted to sacrifice her own life to save other lives. Isn't this concept of individual rights what society is based on today? But those other five people had families too. Maybe they had children. By sacrificing that one person, we could've saved five other lives, saved five other families from the sorrow of death. All the pain that they would've felt, could've been prevented. And to be honest, the grief of five families is indeed more than the grief of one family right?

Now maybe five doesn't seem like a large enough number. So let's make it twenty or maybe a hundred? Now should we choose a single life over multiple lives? Is there a number after which you say, 'This number is large enough to sacrifice one person for'? Is there a tipping point which just goes from 'This person has rights and we should respect these rights' to 'No, these rights don't matter because too many lives are at stake'? And if there does exist such a number, then what is it?

Utilitarianism is a philosophical ideology that believes in actions that lead to maximum good to maximum people and minimize suffering. Utilitarianism believes in the greater good. For some policy or some action to be moral or just, you basically have to do a little mathematical calculation and add up the benefits and subtract the disadvantages or the costs, and the action is just if it maximizes benefits over costs. So although utilitarianism is talking about maximum good, it is crude because it is absolutist in the sense that everything becomes a mathematical equation. So a utilitarian will definitely choose the five lives. Also to a utilitarian, it does not matter if the donor was voluntary or not. What matters is that five lives were saved in lieu of one. It is the final outcome that defines an action as moral or immoral, not the means. In layman terms, utilitarianism says that the ends justify the means.

Utilitarianism is opposed to the concept of individual rights. Now, some philosophers reject utilitarianism saying that people have a right to decide what they do with themselves, and if they want to make a sacrifice for the supposed greater good. All these philosophers had different arguments to support individual rights. So what is our modern defence for individual rights? I think to some extent at a personal level, we don't feel the need to defend them because we take them so much for granted. By using the term 'fundamental' we have ingrained in the minds of the people that having these rights is the first step towards humanity. We believe rights to be a necessary part of modern civilization. We don't question it. Moreover, we expect it. The absence of these rights seems crude and inhumane. It reminds us of some of the darkest periods of history such as Hitler's regime, Stalin's purges and the Reign of Terror. Each is an example where individual rights were violated with excuse of the greater good. Having these rights has become our safeguard against exactly those who wish to misuse power in the name of the greater good.

Now we see two different questions here.

First being, is it more important to focus on individual rights or should we be focusing on the greater good?

The second question being, is there an in-between balance or a grey area where utilitarianism is justified in certain cases?

Now, addressing the first question. Today we live in a highly democratic society, where most of us consider democracy the best possible form of government that we have. Democracy is primarily based on the system of rights. We grow up believing that we as people have rights. We are free to make our own decisions. And all this sounds extremely noble and appealing to us. But what happens when our personal rights or our personal decisions come in the way of the greater good?

A simple example—in order to build a highway, certain

houses need to be broken down. The government promises compensation to all the residents staying there. However, the residents refuse. They have the right to refuse. We live in a democracy so people can have the right to be inconsiderate. Because of these few people, thousands of people would be stuck in traffic for hours every single day. Obviously, it is in the interest of the greater good to relocate the people living there. To be fair, the people don't want to move because that is their home, that is where they have established their own community. It is only natural that they wouldn't want to shift. But is it fair that thousands of people suffer just because they don't want to move? So should the government force the people to move out or should the government remain quiet? In a democracy, the government isn't in a position to do anything, as it must first protect the rights of its citizens. Democracy ties the hands of the government. Hands that can be used to do a lot of great things. Or hands that can lead to the fall of the nation. Better we tie them. After all, history has told us one too many precautionary tales.

In this situation, what is the better thing to do? Some might say it is selfish of the people living in those houses. They should make this small sacrifice for the betterment of society. But the crux of problem here isn't this particular situation. The question is that does greater good always come before individual rights? Or do individual rights come first? And how do we justify this?

Its seems only fitting that as a species we should be more concerned with the overall well-being of our community. We are small particles, a part of something bigger. We can afford to lose a few for the bigger cause. But doesn't this go against every moral fibre in your body? We as compassionate beings have chosen to recognize each individual as significant. It is our humanity, which leads us to believe that every life is important, equal, and that every individual has a say over his or her own life.

Here we can see the power struggle between practicality and morality. But in some twisted sense, being practical means more of society is happy, and isn't the welfare of society the very aim of morality? This, I suppose, comes down to how you define morality. Going by the dictionary definition, morality means doing the right thing, choosing between good or bad. But then I suppose it depends how you define good and bad. Now amusingly enough, the dictionary that I happened to use defines 'good' as displaying moral virtue.

As we have seen and discussed, it is a vague and controversial argument. I'm sure many of us don't completely believe in any one side of this. We're in between; conflicted between our rational desire to be practical, and progressive and emotional desire to be fair and considerate. Once again, we have a war raging between the heart and the mind. And neither one ever wins.

At an individual level, we probably want to be moral

and we respect those who are. But when we talk about leaders or when we choose people to rule the country, we want people who will do best for the country. What we want, is a utilitarian demand. We want people who will minimize damage, who will take decisions that will lead to maximum good for maximum people. It is just how the world functions.

Imagine society to be a building made of blocks. What we care about is whether the building holds and structure remains intact. Individual blocks are secondary. If sparing a few means that the structure survives, we do so gladly. We humans have chosen to live in a society. We have chosen to live together as social animals. And the curse of utilitarianism is what tags along. To survive as a community, we must think and act in favour of the community. It is a necessary evil.

But what about things like cost-benefit analysis? The Czech Republic had recently held a cost benefit analysis on smoking. They realized that smoking was actually beneficial to the economy. They realized that all the money they spent on health costs for people with diseases caused due to smoking, was actually more than made up for in the taxes they earned on cigarettes. And it wasn't just the taxes. All the people who died at an early age due to smoking, saved the government a lot of money; they saved on the pensions that they would have to pay these people when they turned older—for the diseases that came with old age and health insurance. Also they didn't have to pay for old age homes for all those who died early. So with people dying at the age of 40–50 years, the government didn't have to pay for costs that come with old age. People dying actually benefitted the economy, so why make cigarettes illegal? To be fair, people knew the disadvantages of smoking, the risk it carried and were making their own choices. And all the money that they saved per person that smoked could be used to provide food, shelter, education and health benefits to thousands of other people. But the government had the power to stop these deaths. And it didn't simply because smoking was economical. So does this make the Czech government a good or a bad one?

I suppose at the end of the day, we can't just classify situations into categories saying in this case we adopt utilitarian policy, but in this case we should protect individual rights. Most of us today would come to agree that morality is much more complex than just black and white. We are often faced with decisions we cannot make. But a simple saying goes, 'To gain something, you have to lose something'. In harsher or perhaps more accurate words, the famous Russian dictator Stalin once said, 'One must crack a few eggs in order to make an omelette.' Of course by cracking a few eggs he meant you have to purge a few thousand people a day to keep the nation under check. And went on to use the statement to justify gruesome things. But most leaders across time and space, know and believe what Stalin said to be true. Sometimes you have to make sacrifices for the greater good. I guess it simply comes down to whether the omelette is really worth breaking the egg. Stalin also said that a single death is a tragedy, a million deaths is a statistic. But hey, we're not Stalinists here.

chapter 17

The Age of Equality

*Reason has always existed
but not always in a reasonable form.*
—KARL MARX

We were all little when our parents used to tell us not to judge people by how pretty they are, or by how many things they have. But they loved it when we made friends with intelligent kids or very accomplished kids. I don't know about other people but my parents were always pretty particular about me keeping good company. They always judged my friends on their merit. I suppose merit is substituting what used to be money in society. People say don't judge a person by how fat his wallet is, but it seems okay to judge a person by how fat his résumé is. It's always looked down upon to judge people by how good looking they are, or how much money they have. It's called 'A shallow outlook'.

'The Shudra must not acquire knowledge and it is a sin and a crime to give him education. If the Shudra intentionally listens for committing to memory the Veda, then his ears should be filled with (molten) lead; if he utters the Veda, then his tongue should be cut off.'

The Code of Manu (Manusmrithi, which is still one of the scriptural basis for contemporary Hindu civil law in India) defines Shudra as a term for the lowermost social caste in India, these are people who have had no right to education, no right to stay in the same locality as the higher castes, no right to even look at upper caste people in the eye. So today, when we compare these people to others, how can we expect them to compete, to live in a world where others have an advantage, so enormous, over them? If these people are thrown into the world without any skills and any education, how can they survive? How can you throw a person who has never even been in water into the ocean with all others who are well-prepared and proficient swimmers? Moreover, how can you compare him to others around him? How can you expect the one without the ability to swim to even keep his head above water, leave alone be at par with the others? Can he really compete in a system, however fair, of meritocracy? Meritocracy is the system of awarding on the basis of merit; on the basis of capability. The idea of meritocracy was meant to be fair. It was introduced so that every individual has an equal opportunity to excel and do well economically and socially. However, one idea that was tremendously overlooked was that, how can you expect people to have equal opportunity when everyone has a different history, and often it is their situation through history that prevents them from competing in a world where others are way ahead than they are. Society cannot rely on meritocracy alone and in order to establish social equality and justice, there must be reservation for socially suppressed castes and classes.

How can the world expect the child of a pauper, whose father toils to fill the grumbling stomachs in the house, to compete with the son of a wealthy business tycoon who provides every resource to his child to help him succeed? Here it doesn't matter which child is more proficient, the fact is that the wealthier, educated and powerful class does have an advantage even within this system that we call fair and impartial. Like in a race if one person has a massive head start, it won't matter who is faster, the one with the head start is guaranteed to win. If we take the broader picture into sight, where we compare meritocracy to other systems of hierarchy and advantage, it is undeniably the fairest and most reasonable method of rewarding. But meritocracy is not the answer. It is not the solution. But then the question arises, what is? The solution isn't a simple answer. We can't say that because meritocracy isn't the answer, maybe it's democracy or aristocracy. There is always place for modification. Jeans come in standard sizes but it doesn't mean we have to wear them like they are. We have to get them altered according to how they fit us best. There is always room for alteration. In the same way, the answer isn't pure meritocracy. It is meritocracy along with some advantages for the under-privileged.

In India where there is a caste system, those who are considered 'lower caste' are suppressed and have been at the lower end of the totem pole of opportunity for a major portion of Indian history. Even today, when we consider ourselves to be creatures of forward thinking and beyond bias, the truth is, we are still bound by the chains and shackles of prejudice and the system of hierarchy, which ties us to our past of injustice. It is ingrained so deep in the minds of many Indians that those considered Scheduled Castes or Scheduled Tribes are assumed to be inferior. This is why it is important that we today privilege them in some way. Years of starvation, illiteracy, and lower end jobs are scars that won't just heal if people's mindset changes. If one fine day people stop being prejudiced against them, it won't help. What they need, is support and backing up to become level with other people. As Vivek Singh so rightly point's out in his article, 'Social Shift for Upward Mobility'—'I hate to profile people on their birth attributes—like caste, language, colour of skin, region. People should be judged on what they have achieved like education, courtesy, vision, work, rather than what they are born with. But there is no denying of the fact that in past, atrocities have been committed based on birth attributes. And to neutralize the atrocities of the past, we have to provide them a future. It is a moral commitment for us.'

Reservation is just a way for us to help give these people an opportunity where they would be otherwise pushed down. It is a route for them from which they escape the caste barrier. The idea of reserving seats in schools, colleges and jobs isn't something that should last forever. People shouldn't have to be classified into categories such as Scheduled Castes. The idea is simply to let these people emerge and gain equal status in our community. A chance for them to live life like any other. Now, one argument that may come through is that India is a secular state and the Constitution prohibits governance on the basis of class, religion and castes. However, does this mean we ignore the fact that for years these castes have been tortured and crushed? We need to provide an extra incentive to let them bloom again. If we don't help them come up now, they will remain at the bottom for years to come. Instead of running away from the fact that there is caste distinction in India, Indians have to face it head on. Ignoring the fact won't remove caste distinction, it will simply make sure that the people who have suffered because they belong to the so called 'backward castes' will continue to be a step behind other Indians. Because they were treated as socially backward, they have become economically weaker. When we had to create a distinction between castes and they were suffering, no one said, 'We don't want caste distinction.' But now when the government is trying to help them, trying to improve their lives, how come everyone is standing up and saying, 'This is caste differentiation.' This contradicts the idea of justice.

Like Singh says, it is a moral commitment on our part to neutralize the effects of past atrocities. Meritocracy is the method used all over the world now, and is regarded as being one of the best. But we mustn't forget that in any system, there is always a section of society that doesn't benefit. It is up to judgement, and to keep in mind that all factors must be weighed. So we should try to provide them a way to surface—in this case, it was reservation but there might be other ways. It is time for us not only to change how we think, but to show it through actions. Let's stop living in a society where somebody else is called inferior. This is the age of equality.